Navigation at Sea

Compiled by Alfred Hossack

Edited by Lt-Cdr W Sewell MRIN RNR

System by Mentor Textbooks

LUTTERWORTH PRESS
Luke House Farnham Road
Guildford Surrey

Training Notes.

This book has been compiled mainly for the benefit of small boat owners, but it will also serve as a useful introductory to those studying for Masters and Mates qualifications and to those intending to take RYA/DTI Yacht Masters Certificates. Since it is self-correcting it is ideally suited to those working on their own. For this reason it may also recommend itself to teachers who wish to provide students with remedial work, revision courses or pre-course study material.

Three-way text
This text may be used in three different ways, according to the need of the reader or the judgement of the teacher or training officer.
1. General study or selective study. Readers work through the whole text, or through selected sections of the course (see Contents page).
2. Revision. Readers use the text as a self-tester, working through the exercises at the foot of each page and studying the instructional matter only when they have been stopped or branched as the result of an error.
3. Reference. Readers may refer to any particular subject aspect by looking up the index at the back of the book.

Testing procedures
Testing is continuous throughout the book. No reader can complete the text until he (or she) has answered every question correctly.

Proficiency grading at a glance
The Mentor system does away with the need for marking or work correction. But it is recommended that readers jot down, on a work record sheet, each *attempted* three-figure solution they produce. Then they—or their instructor—can award a grading at a glance on the basis of the number of attempts required to complete the course. A suggested marking scheme is laid out on the final working page. A sample Work Record Sheet is available to those ordering this text in quantity.

Immediate diagnosis of difficulties
A Master Sheet is also available to those ordering this text in quantity. This sheet gives the correct solutions and branch solutions, in working sequence, as well as the subject matter. By relating the Master Sheet to any individual Work Record Sheet, areas of difficulty can be detected immediately.

ISBN 0 7188 2132 7

Set reference: 1/3a/5

First published in Great Britain 1974

The traverse tables at the back of this
book have been reproduced from Norie's
Nautical Tables by permission of Imray
Laurie Norie and Wilson Ltd of Wych
House, Saint Ives, Huntingdonshire.

Titles in this series:
Navigation at Sea
Coastal Navigation

MENTOR ENGLISH BOOKS:
Improve your punctuation
Express yourself correctly
Express yourself concisely
Express yourself with power

MENTOR ACCOUNTANCY BOOKS:
Ledger Accounts
Final Accounts

MENTOR METRIC BOOKS:
An Introduction to Metric
Applications of Metric

MENTOR ECONOMICS BOOKS:
Supply and Demand
The Firm and the Market

Printed in Great Britain by Wightman & Co. Ltd.
1-3 Brixton Road, London, SW9 6DS

Contents.

How to use this book

1. Start on the following page. Like all working pages in this book, it has a three-figure number at the top. All page numbers are in ascending order (100, 200, 300, etc.) but many page numbers are missing.

2. Read what the page has to say. Then look at the questions.

3. Choose ONE of the three possible answers against Question A—and note the special number at the end of the answer you choose. Then do the same with Question B. Then do the same with Question C.

4. You now have a three-figure number. Look for a page with this number in the book.

5. If there is a page with the number you have found, resume work on that page. If there is no page with your number, then do the exercise again until you do find a page with your number.

If you jot down on a sheet of paper each three-figure solution you obtain—right or wrong—you will be able to award yourself performance marks at the end. This will also ensure that you do not lose your place as you work through the book.

Start here.

You want to sail from point F (From) to point T (To). If you can see point T before you start, there is no problem. You simply steer, allowing for wind, current, and tidal stream, towards point T—provided there are no obstacles or hazards in the way.

Chartwork or calculation?

But when you cannot see point T before you start, you obviously need to plot both F and T on a chart that covers the area. You then draw a straight line between them—and this line FT will be your True Course to steer.

If you are navigating near land, then you will certainly want a large scale chart that gives the exact location of lights, landmarks, hazards and so forth, together with a lot of other detailed local information. On such a chart you can navigate accurately with the aid of a pencil, parallel rulers (or set squares), a pair of dividers and, of course, a compass.

But suppose you want to make a sea passage of 50 miles or more, a passage that takes you out of sight of land and well clear of any natural hazards such as rocks or sand banks. To carry a series of large scale area charts along your course would be pointless—they would show nothing of value to you. The charts you will need will be those that extend at least between your point of departure and your next expected landfall. This means that they will be *smaller in scale* than the average local chart.

The smaller the scale, the greater the need for accuracy. For example, an error of 1° in True Course may not matter much over four miles, but it will certainly make a difference over forty miles or four hundred miles. So, for ocean sailing, you will need to navigate by mathematical calculation because it is more accurate.

But you will still plot your course on a chart for many reasons. The most obvious reason, perhaps, is to check that your course makes sense.

Choose the correct answer to each of the following.

	dangerous	**1**
A. You would like to sail due West from New York to California. This course is . . .	possible	**4**
	impossible	**7**

---

	possible	**2**
B. You would like to sail due East from New York to Portugal. This course is . . .	impossible	**5**
	dangerous	**8**

---

	impossible	**3**
C. The weather is bad. Your present course will take you through a narrow, rocky channel. This course is . . .	safe	**6**
	dangerous	**9**

You chose the wrong answer to all three questions in the last exercise—and you made exactly the same mistake in each of them.

Either you did not read the lesson or else you feel that vertical lines should measure the vertical distances. Take a graduated rule for a moment and lay it *horizontally* before you.

Look at the vertical graduation lines on the rule. Do you measure along these lines? No—you measure *across* these lines or *between* these lines.

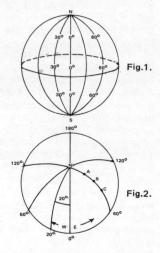

Fig.1.

Fig.2.

And it is just the same with meridians of longitude. They run N-S but they are used for measuring distances E-W.

These distances are expressed in terms of angle—the angle formed by each meridian with the Greenwich meridian (0°) at the Poles.

Moving clockwise between 0° and 180°, all meridians are said to be W (west from Greenwich). Moving anti-clockwise between 0° and 180°, all meridians are said to be E (east from Greenwich).

The first meridian shown to the west of Greenwich here forms an angle of 20° with the Greenwich meridian at the North Pole. So *any* point along this meridian is 20° W.

Now tackle the repeat exercise below.

Choose the correct answer to each of the following.

A. In figure 2 above, A is somewhere along a meridian . . .

60° North	**1**
60° East	**5**
60° West	**6**

B. In figure 2 above, B is somewhere along a meridian . . . .

60° North	**2**
60° West	**4**
60° East	**9**

C. In figure 2 above, C is somewhere along a meridian . . .

60° East	**3**
60° West	**7**
60° North	**8**

You have failed to grasp an important point.

You chose the wrong answer to question C in the last exercise. You got your D.Long figure correct, but you got the *direction* wrong.

Let's look at this problem of crossing the 180° meridian again.

Suppose you are on meridian 178°E and you are approaching the 180° meridian. You are sailing from an easterly longitude to a *more* easterly longitude. So your D.Long must be easterly (E). As soon as you cross the 180° meridian you are sailing from a westerly longitude to a *less* westerly longitude. So your D.Long must still be easterly (E). So, when you cross the 180° meridian from E towards W, your D.Long will always be E.

The exact opposite applies when you cross the 180° meridian from W towards E.

Now tackle the repeat exercise below.

D.Long=distance E or W in minutes or degrees and minutes.

		110′E	**1**
	True Course: 090° (due E)		
A.	Long (F) 65°35′W	110′W	**8**
	Long (T) 63°45′W		
	What is the D.Long?	150′E	**9**

		526′E	**3**
	True Course: 270° (due W)		
B.	Long (F) 107°44′W	566′W	**4**
	Long (T) 116°30′W		
	What is the D.Long?	526′W	**5**

		320′E	**2**
	True Course: 270° (due W)		
C.	Long (F) 177°50′W	360′W	**6**
	Long (T) 176°50′E		
	What is the D.Long?	320′W	**7**

Correct. Now read on.

We must now think about sailing distance in terms of *nautical miles*. One nautical mile=1853 metres of 6080 feet—longer than a land mile, but that need not worry us. From now on, we shall call a nautical mile simply a 'mile'.

D.Lat=distance N or S in minutes or miles
One minute of latitude (N or S) equals one nautical mile. Since the parallels of latitude *are* parallel, this holds true all over the Earth:

  1′ D.Lat=1mile

So we can use D.Lat to measure N-S distance in minutes *or* miles

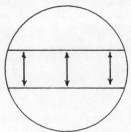

Fig. 4

D.Long=distance E or W in minutes
One minute of longitude (E or W) also equals one mile *along the Equator*. But the meridians of longitude (page 729) are *not* parallel. They converge N and S of the Equator. And so, except at the Equator:

  1′ D.Long=less than 1 mile

So we can use D.Long to measure E-W distance in minutes *but not in miles*.

Departure=distance E or W in miles
We cannot navigate by calculation until we convert E-W distance from minutes to *miles*. This converted distance—now in *miles*—ceases to be D.Long. So we give it a special name. We call it *Departure*.

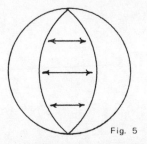

Fig. 5

Except at the Equator, 1′ D.Long is less than one mile.

A. D.Lat is N-S distance expressed in . . .	minutes only	**1**
	miles or minutes	**2**
	miles only	**3**

B. D.Long is E-W distance expressed in . . .	miles only	**5**
	minutes only	**7**
	miles or minutes	**9**

C. Departure is E-W distance expressed in . . .	miles or minutes	**4**
	minutes only	**6**
	miles only	**8**

Correct. Now read on.

By using the meridians of longitude (page 729) and the parallels of latitude (page 593) we can pinpoint the position of any object on the face of the earth.

Pinpointing a position

Let's take a simple example. Suppose you are asked to pinpoint on a map the following ship's position:

    Lat 50°N   ('Lat' is short for 'Latitude')
    Long 6°W   ('Long' is short for 'Longitude')

Pick out the latitude line 50° North of the Equator. Follow along this line until it intersects the longitude line 6° West from Greenwich. And there is your position—a little way off Land's End at the South-West tip of the British Isles.

But we cannot often express positions accurately in whole degrees like this. They nearly always fall *between* degrees N or S and E or W. What do we do then? Do we express each position to the nearest whole degree either way? No! That could mean errors of up to 30 nautical miles.

So each degree (°) is sub-divided into smaller units called *minutes* (′).

There are sixty minutes in every degree.

    1°=60′
    1′=1/60°

Now let's take another example. Pinpoint on a map the following position:

    Lat 33° 52′S   Long 151°13′E

Have you found it yet? It's Sydney, Australia.

If you need to be even more accurate, then sub-divide your minutes by use of decimals. e.g. 1½′ becomes 1·5′.

Look at a map of the world and answer these.

			Rio de Janeiro	**1**
A.	Lat 22°54′S *Where is it?*	Long 43°10′W	West coast of Madagascar	**2**
			Middle of Atlantic Ocean	**3**

			Gulf of Mexico	**4**
B.	Lat 22°33′N *Where is it?*	Long 88°19′E	Calcutta	**6**
			Middle of Indian Ocean	**8**

			Alexandria	**5**
C.	Lat 29°52′S *Where is it?*	Long 31°03′E	Durban	**7**
			South Atlantic Ocean	**9**

You are in the Mediterranean. Your position is Lat 37°50′N Long 20°00′E. You plan to sail to a position Lat 35°10′N Long 20°00′E. In other words, you want to sail due South (180°) and so your longitude will not alter E or W. What is the distance? You plot positions F (From) and T (To) on your chart. You measure the distance between them.

Difference of latitude

Your distance—since you are not altering your longitude E or W—will simply be the *difference of latitude* between Lat 37°50′N and Lat 35°10′N. So, instead of trusting to your accuracy of measurement on a small scale chart, you can simply subtract one latitude position from the other. This difference of latitude—*D.Lat* for short—will be your distance sailed in degrees and minutes:

Lat (F) 37°50′N ⎫ Since you are sailing from a Northerly latitude to a *less*
Lat (T) 35°10′N ⎭ Northerly latitude, your D.Lat is Southerly (S)

D.Lat   2°40′S or 160′S

If you had measured this distance with dividers, your answer would probably have been less accurate than 160′S—it certainly could not have been *more* accurate. Some more examples:

Lat (F) 17°13′N ⎫ Since you are sailing from a Northerly latitude to a *more*
Lat (F) 24°26′N ⎭ Northerly latitude, your D.Lat is Northerly (N)

D.Lat   7°13′N or 433′N

When you are sailing from a latitude North of the Equator to a latitude South of the Equator—or vice versa—then you have to *add* your latitudes:

Lat (F) 3°12′N ⎫ Since you are sailing from a Northerly latitude to a
Lat (T) 1°50′S ⎭ Southerly latitude, your D.Lat is Southerly (S)

D.Lat   5°02′S or 302′S

When you sail due N or due S, your distance=the D.Lat.

A. True Course: 000° (due N)
Lat (F) 41°20′S
Lat (T) 38°30′S
What is the D.Lat or distance?

170′S	**1**
210′N	**4**
170′N	**7**

B. True Course: 180° (due S)
Lat (F) 21°42′S
Lat (T) 25°22′S
What is the D.Lat or distance?

260′S	**3**
220′S	**6**
220′N	**9**

C. True Course: 000° (due N)
Lat (F) 2°55′S
Lat (T) 3°50′N
What is the D.Lat or distance?

405′S	**2**
405′N	**5**
365′N	**8**

Correct. Now read on.

Look at the card of a moderate-sized compass, or at the outer ring of a compass rose on any chart. It is a circle divided into 360 degrees. It is graduated from 0°-359° (360° is the same as 0°). When we give a course to steer we use a three-figure notation. We don't say 5°—we say 005°. We don't say 45°—we say 045°. And so on.

Quadrants of the Compass

The compass splits naturally into four *quadrants* or quarter circles and each quadrant extends through 90°. There are 90° between N and E. 90° between S and E. 90° between S and W. 90° between N and W. When we navigate by calculation, we use tables that express the True Course in quadrantal terms. So let us get used to these quadrants now.

Any course in the N-E quadrant is expressed from N *towards* E. For example:

020° (0+20)=N20°E

Any course in the S-E quadrant is expressed from S *towards* E. For example:

110° (180−70)=S70°E

Any course in the S-W quadrant is expressed from S *towards* W For example:

190° (180+10)=S10°W

Any course in the N-W quadrant is expressed from N *towards.* W. For example:

345° (360−15)=N15°W

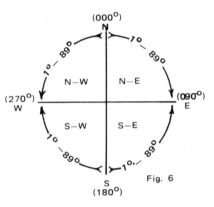

Fig. 6

The four quadrants of the compass: N-E, S-E, S-W, N-W.

A. A ship steers a True Course of 091°. Express this in quadrantal terms.

N91°E	**2**
S89°E	**6**
S01°E	**7**

B. A ship steers a True Course of 269°. Express this in quadrantal terms.

S89°W	**1**
S01°W	**8**
N91°W	**9**

C. A ship steers a True Course of 271°. Express this in quadrantal terms.

N89°W	**3**
N91°W	**4**
S91°W	**5**

Let's look at the right-angled triangle FOT again. To make things simple for ourselves, we will keep it in the *N-E* quadrant (D.Lat=*N*. Departure=*E*).

True Course, Departure and D.Lat

Simple Geometry (or simple common sense) tells us that, when FO=OT, angle OFT=OTF. Since angle FOT= 90°, angle OFT=45°.

So, when D.Lat=Departure, the course to steer from position F to position T must be 045°.

When the Departure is *greater* than the D.Lat, the course to steer will clearly be *greater* than 045°.

When the Departure is *less* than the D.Lat, the course to steer will clearly be *less* than 045°.

In other words, the course to steer in any quadrant is governed by the ratio between Departure and D.Lat.

The ratio is a trigonometrical ratio and can be expressed thus:

$$\frac{\text{Departure}}{\text{D.Lat.}} = \tan(\text{Course})$$

If you don't understand this formula, don't worry. Navigational tables will solve the problem for you.

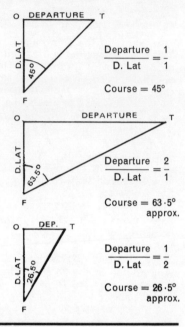

$$\frac{\text{Departure}}{\text{D. Lat}} = \frac{1}{1}$$

Course = 45°

$$\frac{\text{Departure}}{\text{D. Lat}} = \frac{2}{1}$$

Course = 63·5° approx.

$$\frac{\text{Departure}}{\text{D. Lat}} = \frac{1}{2}$$

Course = 26·5° approx.

When Departure=D.Lat, course angle=45°.

	045°	**4**
A. D.Lat is 200 miles N. Departure is 200 miles E. What is the True Course?	063.5°	**6**
	026.5°	**8**

	063.5°	**5**
B. D.Lat is 100 miles N. Departure is 200 miles E. What is the true Course?	045°	**7**
	026.5°	**9**

	045°	**1**
C. D.Lat is 200 miles N. Departure is 100 miles E. What is the True Course?	026.5°	**2**
	063.5°	**3**

You have failed to grasp an important point.

You chose the wrong answer to all three questions in the last exercise—and you made exactly the same mistake in each of them. In each case you forgot to put your D.Long into minutes ('). Let's work through the example once again. Here, to remind you, is the formula for converting D.Long to Departure:

Departure= Difference of longitude × the cosine of the latitude

Or to put it more briefly:

Departure= D.Long cos (lat)

A ship sails due E along latitude 60°N, from Long 22°00′W to Long 21°00′W. What is the Departure (i.e. the distance in miles)?

D.Long = (Long 22°00′W—Long 21°00′W) = 1°E = 60′E
Cos 60° = 0.5
So Departure = 60 × 0.5 miles E
           = 30 miles E

If we had failed to express the D.Long in minutes and had left it in degrees, our answer would have been 1 × 0.5 miles E = 0.5 miles E. This would be impossible. A D.Long of 60′ could only reduce to 0.5 miles near the North Pole or South Pole.

Now tackle the repeat exercise below.

Departure= D.Long × the cosine of the latitude.

A. A ship sails between positions: Lat 41°24′S Long 19°00′W (From) Lat 41°24′S Long 20°00′W (To) So it sails along Lat 41°24′S. Cosine of 41°24′=0.75. What is the Departure?	0.75 miles W 45 miles E 45 miles W	**2** **5** **8**
B. A ship sails between positions: Lat 53°06′S Long 20°00′W (From) Lat 53°06′S Long 19°00′W (To) So it sails along Lat 53°06′S. Cosine of 53°06′=0.6 What is the Departure?	36 miles W 0.6 miles E 36 miles E	**1** **4** **7**
C. A ship sails between positions: Lat 00°00′ Long 20°00′W (From) Lat 00°00′ Long 19°00′W (To) So it sails along Lat 0° (Equator). Cosine of 0°=1. What is the Departure?	60 miles W 1 mile E 60 miles E	**3** **6** **9**

So Departure is distance E or W expressed in miles (page 157). Or we can say Departure is D.Long *converted* to miles.

Converting D.Long to Departure
The further N or S we go, the closer the meridians of longitude become. The closer the meridians of longitude become, the smaller the Departure. At Lat 0° (the Equator), 1′ D.Long=1 mile exactly. At Lat 20° (N or S), 1′ D.Long= 0.9397 miles. At Lat 40° (N or S), 1′ D.Long=0.766 miles. And so on. In other words there is a ratio between D.Long and Departure *which varies with the latitude*. This ratio is expressed in the following formula:

Departure=Difference of longitude×the cosine of the latitude

Or to put it more briefly:

Departure=D.Long cos (lat)

So, if we are sailing along a parallel of latitude, we can look up the cosine of that latitude in any tables that give us the 'Natural Functions of Angles'. We then multiply this by our D.Long to get our distance in miles. An example:

A ship sails due E along latitude 60°N, from Long 22°00′W to Long 21°00′W. What is the Departure (i.e. the distance in miles)?

D.Long = (Long 22°00′W − Long 21°00′W)=1°E=60′E
Cos 60° = 0.5

So Departure=60×0.5 miles E
= 30 miles E

The above formula is a trigonometrical formula. If you are not interested in trigonometry, it doesn't matter. When you navigate at sea, you use a book of tables where all the trigonometical calculations are already done for you. But more of that later.

Departure=D.Long × the cosine of the latitude.

A.	A ship sails between positions: Lat 41°24′S Long 19°00′W (From) Lat 41°24′S Long 20°00′W (To) So it sails along Lat 41°24′S. Cosine of 41°24′=0.75. What is the Departure?	0.75 miles W	**2**
		45 miles E	**5**
		45 miles W	**8**
B.	A ship sails between positions: Lat 53°06′S Long 20°00′W (From) Lat 53°06′S Long 19°00′W (To) So it sails along Lat 53°06′S. Cosine of 53°06′=0.6 What is the Departure?	36 miles W	**1**
		0.6 miles E	**4**
		36 miles E	**7**
C.	A ship sails between positions: Lat 00°00′ Long 20°00′W (From) Lat 00°00′ Long 19°00′W (To) So it sails along Lat 0° (Equator). Cosine of 0°=1. What is the Departure?	60 miles W	**3**
		1 mile E	**6**
		60 miles E	**9**

The traverse table is easy to use—once you get accustomed to its layout. Put a marker in this page so that you can return to it. Now look at the specimen traverse pages at the back of the book. Study them carefully.

Layout of the traverse table

You will see that each traverse table page is a double page—this is to allow space for Distance figures from 1 to 600 miles. You will also see that each page is 'numbered' by means of angles and that there are *two* angles on each page.

Each angle represents a True Course to steer within one of the four quadrants of the compass. The small 'arrowed' figures at the top and bottom are designed to help you convert each quadrant reading to a three-figure notation reading (page 217).

Each page provides figures for *two* quadrant Courses—the Course angle shown at the top and the Course angle shown at the bottom. When you are concerned with the Course angle at the *top,* you read the columns *downwards.* When you are concerned with the Course angle at the *bottom,* you read the columns *upwards.*

Note that the two angles on any one page add up to 90°—they are in fact complementary angles. Note that what is *D.Lat* reading *downwards* is *Departure* reading *upwards.* Note that what is *Departure* reading *downwards* is *D.Lat* reading *upwards.*

There is a reason for this and, if you are interested, you can look at page 452 again and work it out for yourself (30° and 60° are complementary angles). If you can't understand the reason, it doesn't matter at all.

At the top and bottom of each column you will also see *D.Long* and *Dep* printed in italics and bracketed together. Ignore these for the moment.

Choose the correct answer in each of these.

A.	Find the traverse table for 30°. Look in the 'Distance' column for 400 (=400 miles). What are the figures against 400 for D.Lat and Departure?	D.Lat=200.0 Dep =346.4	**3**
		D.Lat=346.4 Dep =200.0	**4**
		D.Lat=346.4 Dep =346.4	**5**
B.	Find the traverse table for 60°. Look in the 'Distance' column for 400 (=400 miles). What are the figures against 400 for D.Lat and Departure?	D.Lat=346.4 Dep =200.0	**1**
		D.Lat=200.0 Dep =346.4	**8**
		D.Lat=200.0 Dep =200.0	**9**
C.	The angle at the top of a traverse table page is 45°. What will be the angle at the bottom of the same page?	45 degrees	**2**
		0 degrees	**6**
		90 degrees	**7**

Correct. Now read.

There are times when the traverse table fails to provide the figure we need. Here are some points to note.

When the Lat or M.Lat is not a whole number

Latitudes and mean latitudes seldom oblige us by being whole numbers. So, when we are converting D.Long to Departure (or vice versa), we must look up the latitude angle above and below:

M.Lat is 29°15′. D.Long is 320′. What is the Departure?

At M.Lat 29° and D.Long 320, Departure=279.9 miles
At M.Lat 30° and D.Long 320, Departure=277.1 miles

So a difference of 1° M.Lat produces a difference of 2.8 miles Departure.
So a difference of 15′ M.Lat produces a difference of 0.7 miles Departure.
So Departure=279.9 – 0.7=279.2 miles

When the D.Long exceeds 600′

When we are converting D.Long to Departure (or vice versa), we sometimes find that the figure we are looking for exceeds the limit of the traverse table. When this happens, we must divide the required figure by 2 or 3 or some other convenient number first—and then multiply up again afterwards:

M.Lat is 61°. Departure is 320 miles. What is the D.Long?

When the latitude angle is 61°, the figures in the Departure column cease at 290.9 (see traverse table pages at back). So divide the 320 Departure by 2 and look up the D.Long:

At M.Lat 61°, Departure 160=D.Long 330′
Now multiply by 2:
At M.Lat 61°, Departure 320=D.Long 660

Use the traverse pages at the back to answer these.

A. M.Lat=30°20′
D.Long=140′
Find the Departure.

Dep=120.8 miles **5**

Dep=120.96 miles **7**

Dep=70.7 miles **9**

B. M.Lat=59°00′
Departure=310 miles
Find the D.Long.

D.Long=301′ **4**

D.Long=602′ **6**

D.Long=362′ **8**

C. M.Lat=29°00′
D.Long=640′
Find the Departure.

Dep=279.9 miles **1**

Dep=310.2 miles **2**

Dep=559.8 miles **3**

You have failed to grasp an important point.

You chose the wrong answer to all three questions in the last exercise—and you made exactly the same mistake in each of them.

In each case you carried out your subtractions on a decimal base, forgetting that there are only *sixty* minutes in one degree. Let's take a further example:

Lat (F) 37°20′N ⎫ Since you are sailing from a Northerly latitude to a
Lat (T) 34°30′N ⎬ less Northerly latitude, your D.Lat is Southerly (S).

To find your D.Lat you must subtract the smaller latitude from the larger latitude. This means subtracting 30′ from 20′ and this, in turn, means 'borrowing' 1° and turning it into 60′. You now subtract 30′ from 80′ (20′+60′):

D.Lat=2°50′S or 170′S

Now tackle the repeat exercise below.

When you sail due N or due S, your distance=the D.Lat.

A.
True Course: 000° (due N)
Lat (F) 41°20′S
Lat (T) 38°30′S
What is the D.Lat or distance?

170′S	**1**
210′N	**4**
170′N	**7**

B.
True Course: 180° (due S)
Lat (F) 21°42′S
Lat (T) 25°22′S
What is the D.Lat or distance?

260′S	**3**
220′S	**6**
220′N	**9**

C.
True Course: 000° (due N)
Lat (F) 2°55′S
Lat (T) 3°50′N
What is the D.Lat or distance?

405′S	**2**
405′N	**5**
365′N	**8**

Another look at the right-angled triangle FOT. To make things simple, we will still keep it in the *N-E* quadrant (D.Lat=*N*. Departure=*E*).

Distance, True Course and D.Lat

When angle OFT=60°, FT will always be *twice* the length of FO.

So, when the True Course is 60°, the Distance will be *twice* the D.Lat.

In other words, there is a ratio between Distance and D.Lat that depends upon the True Course. This ratio is a trigonometrical ratio and can be expressed thus:

D.Lat=Distance×cos (Course)

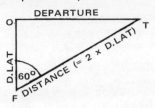

Distance, True Course and Departure

When angle OFT=30°, FT will always be *twice* the length of OT. So, when the True Course is 30°, the Distance will be *twice* the Departure.

In other words, there is a ratio between Distance and Departure that depends upon the True Course. This ratio is a trigonometrical ratio and can be expressed thus:

Departure=Distance×sin (Course)

If you don't understand these formulae, don't worry. Navigational tables will solve the problem for you.

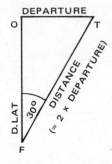

Choose the correct answers in each of these.

---

		800 miles	**3**
A.	True Course is 120° (S60°E). D.Lat is 200 miles. What is the Distance?	100 miles	**6**
		400 miles	**9**

---

		100 miles	**1**
B.	True Course is 240° (S60°W). D.Lat is 200 miles. What is the Distance?	400 miles	**4**
		1,600 miles	**7**

		2,200 miles	**2**
C.	True Course is 330° (N30°W). Departure is 200 miles. What is the Distance?	400 miles	**5**
		100 miles	**8**

The angle between a N-S line and an E-W line must be 90°. So our navigation calculations can all be solved by means of a right-angled triangle FOT. FO is the distance N or S in miles (D.Lat). OT is the distance E or W in miles (Departure). FT is the distance travelled on a rhumb line course to get from position F to position T. The angle OFT is the angle to steer along the rhumb line course FT.

Quadrant and True Course

The angle OFT is an angle in one the four quadrants of the compass (page 217). So, before we can express this angle in terms of a True Course to steer, we must realise what quadrant we are in. Suppose the angle OFT is 45°:

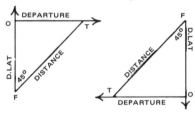 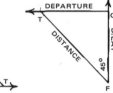

D.Lat is *N*.	D.Lat is *S*.	D.Lat is *S*.	D.Lat is *N*.
Departure is *E*.	Departure is *W*.	Departure is *E*.	Departure is *W*.
So quadrant of	So quadrant of	So quadrant of	So quadrant of
compass is *N-E*.	compass is *S-W*.	compass is *S-E*.	compass is *N-W*.
So True Course	So True Course	So True Course	So True Course
= N45°E	= S45°W	= S45°E	= N45°W
= 045°	= 225°	= 135°	= 315°

Choose the correct answer in each of these.

	210°	**2**
A. D.Lat is S. Departure is W. The quadrant angle to steer is 30° What is the True Course?	030°	**6**
	240°	**7**

	300°	**3**
B. D.Lat is N. Departure is W. The quadrant angle to steer is 30° What is the True Course?	330°	**4**
	030°	**5**

	150°	**1**
C. D.Lat is S. Departure is E. The quadrant angle to steer is 30°. What is the True Course?	030°	**8**
	120°	**9**

Correct. Now read on.

We have just seen that the angles at the top and bottom of a traverse table can represent a Course to steer within one of the quadrants of the compass. Now let us see how to use the table.

Traverse table angles as True Course

You intend to sail for 301 miles on a True Course of 031°. What will be the Departure and the D.Lat?

031°=N31°E. So look for 31° in the traverse table pages (at back of book). Look for 301 miles in the Distance column. Read off against 301 to find your Departure and D.Lat. Since your Course is *N31°E*, your D.Lat will be *N* and your Departure will be *E*:

    Departure=155 miles E
    D.Lat   =258 miles N

You intend to sail from position F to position T. The Departure is 282.5 miles E. The D.Lat is 170 miles (or minutes) N. What is the Distance and the True Course to steer?

Look in the traverse table pages until you find 282.5 Departure and 170 D.Lat *together*. The traverse table page with 59° gives you 282.9 Departure and 170 D.Lat against Distance 330. This is close enough for all practical purposes. So (since your D.Lat is *N* and your Departure is *E*):

    Distance   =330 miles
    True Course =N59°E=059°

There are forty-five double pages in the traverse table, but there is no need to scour all through them to find the one with the right Course angle. We have already seen (page 241) that, when the ratio of Departure to D.Lat is 1:1, the course angle will be 45° and that, when the ratio of Departure to D.Lat is 2:1, the course angle will be 63.5°. The ratio here (282.9 : 170) is rather less than 2:1. So the angle we are looking for must be in the region of 57°-61°.

Choose the correct answer in each of these.

A. True Course=210°
Distance=500 miles
Find the D.Lat and the Departure.

    D.Lat=250 miles S
    Dep =433 miles W **5**

    D.Lat=433 miles S
    Dep =250 miles W **7**

    D.Lat=3031 miles S
    Dep =1750 miles W **9**

B. D.Lat=492 miles N
Departure=295.8 miles E
Find the True Course and Distance.

    True Course=059°
    Dist=574 miles **1**

    True Course =149°
    Dist=574 miles **2**

    True Course=031°
    Dist=574 miles **3**

C. D.Lat=251 miles S
Departure=453 miles W
Find the True Course and Distance.

    True Course=241°
    Dist=518 miles **4**

    True Course=061°
    Dist=518 miles **6**

    True Course=209°
    Dist=518 miles **8**

You chose the wrong answer to questions B and C in the last exercise—and you made exactly the same mistake in each of them. These were the ones dealing with the procedure for converting D.Long to Departure (or vice versa) when the D.Long exceeds 600′. Let's go through it again.

When we are converting D.Long to Departure (or vice versa) we sometimes find that the figure we are looking for exceeds the limit of the traverse table. When this happens, we must divide the required figure by 2 or 3 or some other convenient number first—and then multiply up again afterwards:

M.Lat is 61°. Departure is 320 miles. What is the D.Long?

When the latitude angle is 61°, the figures in the Departure column cease at 290.9 (see traverse table pages at back). So divide the 320 Departure by 2 and look up the D.Long:

At M.Lat 61°, Departure 160=D.Long 330

Now—*and this is what you forgot to do*—multiply by 2 (because you originally divided by 2):

At M.Lat 61°, Departure 320=D.Long 660′

Now tackle the repeat exercise below.

Use the traverse pages at the back to answer these.

A. M.Lat=30°20′ D.Long=140′ Find the Departure.	Dep=120.8 miles **5** Dep=120.96 miles **7** Dep=70.7 miles **9**	

| **B.** M.Lat=59°00′
Departure=310 miles
Find the D.Long. | D.Long=301′ **4**
D.Long=602′ **6**
D.Long=362′ **8** | |

| **C.** M.Lat=29°00′
D.Long=640′
Find the Departure. | Dep=279.9 miles **1**
Dep=310.2 miles **2**
Dep=559.8 miles **3** | |

We have not talked of celestial navigation because this is a separate subject in itself. We have not talked of time and speed (1 knot=1 nautical mile per hour) but we have introduced these into the additional navigation exercises that you will find at the back of the book.

At the back you will also find a subject index. So you may now use this book for reference whenever you wish.

If you would like to check your own performance on this course, here is a simple way to do it.

Look at the record sheet on which you have written down all your attempted three-figure solutions. If you completed the course in only 24 attempts, give yourself full marks. If you took more than 24 attempts, then deduct 5 marks for each extra attempt. Like this:

Number of attempts	Percentage marks	Grading letter
24	100%	A
25	95%	A
26	90%	A
27	85%	A
28	80%	B
29	75%	B
30	70%	B
31	65%	B
32	60%	C
33	55%	C
34	50%	C
35	45%	C
36	40%	D
37	35%	D
38	30%	D
39	25%	D
40	20%	E
41	15%	E
42	10%	E
43	5%	E
(44 or more)	0%	F

Correct. Now read on.

Imagine you are at the North Pole with a miraculous drill. You bore a narrow shaft downwards, through the Earth's centre, to the South Pole. Now you march southwards along the Greenwich meridian (page 100) until you reach a halfway point between the two Poles—and you bore another shaft through to the Earth's centre. The angle between this halfway shaft and your Polar shaft will be 90°.

Now you march due West (or due East) around the world, boring further shafts to the Earth's centre. Now you trace an imaginary circle round the Earth joining all these shaft holes.

Parallels of latitude

This imaginary circle is called the 'Equator' because it divides the globe into two equal half-spheres: a Northern hemisphere and a Southern hemisphere. You mark this circle 0° (zero degrees).

Now march halfway N to the North Pole and bore another shaft to the Earth's centre. The angle of this shaft to the Equator will be 45°N of the Equator. Now march due West (or due East) and make another circle round the Earth.

Any point along this circular line will be 45° of the Equator.

Carry on making these circular lines above and below the Equator. Note that they get smaller and smaller as they get further N and S—until, at the Poles, they become mere dots.

Each circle marks a position North or South of the Equator. And all the circles are parallel with one another. That is why they are called *parallels of latitude*.

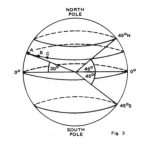

Fig. 3

Choose the correct answer to each of these.

A.	In figure 3 above, A is somewhere along a position line . . .	30° North	**1**
		30° West	**8**
		30° South	**9**

B.	In figure 3 above, B is somewhere along a position line . . .	30° South	**2**
		30° North	**6**
		30° West	**7**

C.	In figure 3 above, C is somewhere along a position line . . .	30° North	**3**
		30° West	**4**
		30° South	**5**

The most convenient course to steer a ship is a steady course so that the bearing of the ship's head stays constant. If you steer a steady course, then your track will cut all meridians (page 729) at the same angle.

Sailing along a meridian
If your True Course is 000° (due N) or 180° (due S) you will be sailing along a meridian of longitude. The angle between your course and any meridian will then be 0°.

Sailing along a parallel
If your True Course is 090° (due E) or 270° (due W) you will be sailing along a parallel of latitude. The angle between your course and any meridian will then be 90°.

Rhumb Line or Plain Sailing
But, if you want to sail from position F to position T, it is most unlikely that your True Course will be 000°, 090°, 180° or 270°. Suppose your required course is 045° (N45°E)—then your course will cut the meridians at an angle of 45°.

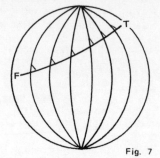

Fig. 7

A line on the Earth's surface that cuts all meridians at the same angle is called a *rhumb line*. And sailing along a rhumb line is called *rhumb line sailing* or, more simply, *plain sailing*.

Rhumb line—a line that cuts all meridians at the same angle.

A ship's True Course is **A.** 112° (S68°E). The ship is sailing along . . .	a parallel	**4**
	a rhumb line	**6**
	a meridian	**8**
A ship's True Course is **B.** 193° (S13°W). The ship is sailing along . . .	a meridian	**1**
	a rhumb line	**2**
	a parallel	**3**
A ship's True Course is **C.** 290° (N70°W). The ship is sailing along . . .	a meridian	**5**
	a parallel	**7**
	a rhumb line	**9**

Correct. Now read on.

We already know the formula for converting D.Long (E-W distance in minutes) to Departure (E-W distance in miles). We used it on page 278:

Departure = D.Long × the cosine of the latitude

When we are sailing due E or due W, our latitude will remain unchanged and so we simply look up the cosine of that latitude. But, when we sail on a *rhumb line* course, our *latitude is changing all the time.* So, before we can look up the cosine of the latitude, we must ask ourselves *"Which* latitude?"

Departure and Mean Latitude

Suppose you are sailing along the rhumb line course FT in Fig. 8. The meridians Ft and fT are converging. So the distance you travel in an E or W direction cannot be greater than the distance along the parallel Ff. Nor can it be smaller than the distance along the parallel tT.

So your distance E or W must be equal to some parallel lying *between* Ff and tT.

This imagined parallel is known as the 'middle latitude'. The calculations needed to find the middle latitude are slightly involved and, for distances of 600 miles and less, these calculations are unnecessary.

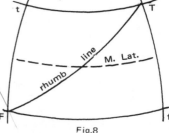

Fig.8

For distances up to 600 miles, the *mean latitude* (M.Lat) is accurate enough for our calculations. So, for distances up to 600 miles, here is the formula we use to find Departure when we are on a rhumb line course:

Departure = D.Long × the cosine of the mean latitude

Choose the correct answer in each of the following.

A. You are sailing between F and T on a course of 090° (due E). To find your Departure, you must multiply your D.Long by the cosine of . . .

the mean latitude **2**

the middle latitude **5**

the latitude you are sailing along **8**

B. You are sailing between F and T on a course of 030° (N30°E). The distance is about 400 to 450 miles. To find your Departure, you must multiply your D.Long by the cosine of . . .

the mean latitude **3**

the middle latitude **6**

the latitude you are sailing along **9**

C. You are sailing between F and T on a course of 030° (N30°E). The distance is about 700 to 800 miles. To find your Departure, you would need to multiply your D.Long by the cosine of . . .

the mean latitude **1**

the middle latitude **4**

the latitude you are sailing along **7**

You are still in the Mediterranean. Your position is 35°00′N 30°40′E. You plan to sail to a position 35°00′N 27°20′E. In other words you want to sail along a parallel of latitude 35°00′N. What is the distance? You plot positions F (From) and T (To) on your chart and you measure between them.

Difference of longitude

Your distance—since you are not altering your latitude N or S—will simply be the *difference of longitude* between 30°40′E and 27°20′E. So, instead of trusting to your accuracy of measurement on a small scale chart, you merely subtract the smaller longitude from the greater. This difference of longitude —*D.Long* for short—will be your distance sailed in terms of minutes or degrees and minutes:

Long (F) 30°40′E ⎱ Since you are sailing from an Easterly longitude to a
Long (T) 27°20′E ⎰ *less* Easterly longitude, your D.Long is Westerly (W).
D.Long   3°20′W   <u>or 200′W</u>

Another example:

Long (F) 101°35′E ⎱ Since you are sailing from an Easterly longitude to a
Long (T) 107°45′E ⎰ *more* Easterly longitude, your D.Long is Easterly (E)
D.Long   6°10′E   or 370′E

If you sail across the 0° or 180° meridian (see page 729) you must *add* your longitudes and, if their sum exceeds 180°, subtract the total from 360°:

Long (F) 178°00′E   ⎫ Since you are sailing from an Easterly longitude to
Long (T) 175°00′W   ⎬ a *more* Easterly longitude and from a Westerly
    353°00′   ⎭ longitude to a *less* Westerly longitude, your D.Long
            is Easterly (E)

D.Long=360°−353°=7°E or 420′E

D.Long=distance E or W in minutes or degrees and minutes.

	True Course: 090° (due E)	110′E	**1**
A.	Long (F) 65°35′W	110′W	**8**
	Long (T) 63°45′W		
	What is the D.Long?	150′E	**9**

	True Course: 270° (due W)	526′E	**3**
B.	Long (F) 107°44′W	566′W	**4**
	Long (T) 116°30′W		
	What is the D.Long?	526′W	**5**

	True Course: 270° (due W)	320′E	**2**
C.	Long (F) 177°50′W	360′W	**6**
	Long (T) 176°50′E		
	What is the D.Long?	320′W	**7**

So, before we can navigate from F to T, we need to pinpoint both positions. A glance at a globe of the world shows that it is covered with a network of imaginary lines. Some are 'vertical'. Some are 'horizontal'.

Meridians of longitude

Let's look at the 'vertical' lines first. Each of these lines runs between the North and South Poles along the shortest possible path. Each line—since the Earth is a sphere—forms a half-circle. Each line is a *meridian of longitude.*

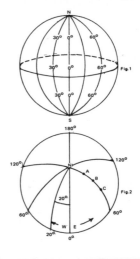

Note the meridian that runs through Greenwich (London) in the British Isles. This is the Greenwich meridian and is marked 0°. Note the meridian opposite the Greenwich meridian. This runs close to New Zealand and is marked 180°.

Now look down upon the North Pole, with the Greenwich meridian directly in front of you. You are looking, in effect, at a plane circle. This circle is graded from 0°—180° *twice*—once working clockwise and once working anti-clockwise from the Greenwich meridian. Every meridian to the left of Greenwich is said to be W (West from Greenwich). Every meridian to the right of Greenwich is said to be E (East from Greenwich).

The first meridian shown to the West of Greenwich here forms an angle of 20° with the Greenwich meridian at the Pole. So *any* point along this line is 20° W.

Fig.1

Fig.2

Choose the correct answer to each of the following.

A.	In figure 2 above, A is somewhere along a meridian . . .	60° North	**1**
		60° East	**5**
		60° West	**6**

B.	In figure 2 above, B is somewhere along a meridian	60° North	**2**
		60° West	**4**
		60° East	**9**

C.	In figure 2 above, C is somewhere along a meridian . . .	60° East	**3**
		60° West	**7**
		60° North	**8**

Correct. Now read on.

3 4

The angles at the top and bottom of a traverse table can also represent mean latitude (M.Lat) or simply latitude (Lat.) Used in this way they enable us to convert D.Long to Departure, or Departure to D.Long, without using formulae.

When we use the traverse table for this purpose, we ignore the ordinary headings—Distance, D.Lat and Departure—entirely. The only two headings that concern us are the italicised headings—*D.Long* and *Departure*—that are linked with brackets.

Note that the italicised *Dep* column is in the centre when one reads downward, but that it is on the right hand side when one reads upwards. Note that the italicised *D.Long* is on the left hand side, whichever way one reads it.

Traverse tables angles as latitude or mean latitude

You intend to sail from position F to position T. The D.Long is 323′E. The M.Lat is 29°. What is the Departure?

M.Lat=29°. So look for 29° in the traverse table pages (at back of book). Find 323 in the *D.Long* column. Look at the figure in the bracketed *Dep* column beside it—and this is the Departure. Since the D.Long is E, the Departure (now in miles) will also be E:

Departure=282.5 miles E.

You intend to sail from position F to position T. The Departure is 155 miles E. The M.Lat is 61°. What is the D.Long?

M.Lat=61°. So look up 61° in the traverse table pages (at back of book). Look for 155 in the *Dep* column. The nearest to 155—and this is good enough for all practical purposes—is 155.1. Look at the figure in the bracketed *D.Long* column beside it—and this is the D.Long. Since the Departure is E, the D.Long (now in minutes) will also be E:

D.Long=320′E.

Choose the correct answers in each of these.

A. D.Long=134′E
M.Lat=30°
What is the Departure?

Dep=67 miles E **3**
Dep=134 miles E **6**
Dep=116 miles E **9**

B. D.Long=140′W
M.Lat=59°
What is the Departure?

Dep=140 miles W **2**
Dep=120 miles W **5**
Dep=72.1 miles W **8**

C. Departure=336 miles E
M.Lat=31°
What is the D.Long

D.Long=288′E **1**
D.Long=173.1′E **4**
D.Long=392′E **7**

Correct. Now read on.

While we are dealing with latitudes, we may as well see how to find the *mean latitude*. Mean latitude plays a very important part in navigation calculations, as we shall shortly see.

Mean latitude

Mean latitude—*M.Lat* for short—is simply the halfway point between any two latitudes. It is an 'average' latitude. The easiest way to find the average between any two quantities is to add them together ánd then divide the result by 2. For example, if a company shows £12,000 profit one year and £8,000 profit the next year, then its average profit will be £20,000÷2=£10,000. It's exàctly the same when we want to find the mean latitude:

Lat (F) 37°50′N ⎫ Add the two latitudes (73°00′) and then divide the
Lat (T) 35°10′N ⎭ result by 2.
M.Lat   36°30′

Commonsense tells us that this M.Lat is 36°30′*N*—but there is no need to bother about N and S with mean latitudes.

Now let's go back to our example of average company profits for a moment. If the company had showed a *loss* of £8,000 in its second year, then we would have to *subtract* the two figures and then divide by 2, giving us an average profit of only £2,000. It's exactly the same when we want to find the mean latitude of one latitude *North* of the Equator and one latitude *South* of the Equator:

Lat (F) 12°00′N ⎫ Subtract one latitude from the other (4°00′) and then
Lat (T) 8°00′S   ⎭ divide the result by 2.
M.Lat   2°00′

A moment's thought will tell us that this M.Lat is 2°00′*N* of the Equator—but there is no need to bother about N or S.

M.Lat is simply the mean or average between two latitudes.

		39°30′ **1**
A. Lat (F) 42°55′N		
Lat (T) 36°45′N		3°05′ **5**
What is the M.Lat?		
		39°50′ **6**

		23°24′ **3**
B. Lat (F) 20°56′S		
Lat (T) 25°52′S		23°04′ **7**
What is the M.Lat?		
		2°28′ **8**

		3°50′ **2**
C. Lat (F) 4°50′S		
Lat (T) 2°50′N		1°00′ **4**
What is the M.Lat?		
		2°00′ **9**

One more step and you will be almost ready to calculate your True Course and distance between any two positions anywhere at sea.

You are still in the Mediterranean. You sail along a rhumb line course from a position 35°08′N 15°50′E to a position 38°28′N 20°00′E. First you calculate your D.Lat (page 167) and your D.Long (page 634):

Lat (F)	35°08′N	Long (F)	15°50′E
Lat (T)	38°28′N	Long (T)	20°00′E
D.Lat	3°20′N=200′N	D.Long	4°10′E=250′E

Distance N or S in miles

Your D.Lat is 200′N. And 1′ D.Lat=1 mile. So you have no problem in expressing your distance N or S in miles:

D.Lat=200 miles N

Distance E or W in miles

Before you can find your Departure (distance E or W in miles) you must first calculate your M.Lat (mean latitude) because as we saw on page 629:

Departure=D.Long × the cosine of the mean latitude

Lat (F)   35°08′N ⎫ Add the two latitudes and divide the result by 2.
Lat (T)   38°28′N ⎭ Direction N or S is unimportant. (Page 765)
M.Lat   36°48′

D.Long=250′E. Cos 36°48′=0.8 (From 'Natural Functions of Angles'). So:

Departure=D.Long × cos (M.Lat)
          =250 × 0.8 miles E
          =200 miles E

We now have our N-S distance in *miles*. And we have our E-W distance in *miles*.

Some more practice with D.Lat, D.Long and M.Lat.

A ship sails between positions:	210′S	**2**
A. 14°45′N 61°40′E (From) 11°55′N 57°50′E (To)	170′S	**4**
What is the D.Lat?	170′N	**9**

	270′W	**3**
B. What is the D.Long?	230′E	**7**
	230′W	**8**

	13°20′	**1**
C. What is the M.Lat?	13°00′	**5**
	26°40′	**6**

You chose the wrong answer to all three questions in the last exercise—and you made exactly the same mistake in each of them.

Either you did not read the lesson or else you feel that horizontal lines should measure horizontal distances. Take a graduated rule for a moment and lay it *vertically* in front of you.

Look at the graduation lines on the rule, each one running horizontally above the other. Do you measure along these lines? No—you measure *across* these lines or *between* these lines.

And it is just the same with parallels of latitude. They run E-W but they are used for measuring distances N-S.

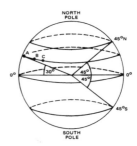

This distance N or S is expressed in terms of angle—the angle formed between any point on the parallel of latitude and the Equator (0°).

The apex of the angle is the Earth's centre.

So, if a parallel of latitude is north of the Equator and makes an angle of 45° with the Equator, then *any* point along that parallel is 45°N. On the other hand, if a parallel of latitude is south of the Equator and makes an angle of 45° with the Equator, then *any* point along that parallel is 45°S.

Fig.3.

Now tackle the repeat exercise below.

Choose the correct answer to each of these.

A. In figure 3 above, A is somewhere along a position line . . .	30° North	**1**
	30° West	**8**
	30° South	**9**
B. In figure 3 above, B is somewhere along a position line . . .	30° South	**2**
	30° North	**6**
	30° West	**7**
C. In figure 3 above, C is somewhere along a position line . . .	30° North	**3**
	30° West	**4**
	30° South	**5**

Correct. Now read on.

8 7 9

If we can convert D.Long to Departure (page 278), we can also convert Departure to D.Long:

Departure = D.Long × cosine of the latitude
So D.Long = Departure ÷ cosine of the latitude
Or (to avoid division):
D.Long. = Departure × secant of the latitude

Converting Departure to D.Long.
It doesn't matter if you don't understand the terms 'cosine' and 'secant'. All you have to do is remember the formula and apply it. An example:

A ship leaves a position Lat 60°00′N Long 20°00′W and sails along a True Course of 270° (due W) for 30 miles. So it sails along Lat 60°N. Find the D.Long and the new position.

D.Long = Departure sec (lat)

So all we need is to look up the secant of the latitude in the 'Natural Functions of Angles' tables—and multiply it by the Departure:

Departure = 30 miles W
Sec 60° = 2
So D.Long = 30 × 2W
= 60′W or 1°W

Now to find the new position. The latitude has not altered. The longitude has increased by 1°W. So:

New position: Lat 60°00′N Long 21°00′W

D.Long = Departure × the secant of the latitude.

A.	A ship leaves a position Lat 48°12′S Long 160°00′W and sails due E for 40 miles. So it sails along Lat 48°12′S. Secant of 48°12′=1.5. What is the new position?	Lat 48°12′S Long 159°00′W	**2**
		Lat 48°12′S Long 159°00′E	**4**
		Lat 48°12′S Long 159°58.5′E	**9**
B.	A ship leaves a position Lat 36°54′N Long 160°00′E and sails due W for 48 miles. So it sails along Lat 36°54′N. Secant of 36°54′=1.25. What is the new position?	Lat 36°54′N Long 159°00′E	**1**
		Lat 36°54′N Long 159°58.75′E	**5**
		Lat 36°54′N Long 159°00′W	**6**
C.	A ship leaves a position Lat 00°00′ Long 160°00′W and sails due E for 60 miles. So it sails along Lat 0°. Secant of 0°=1. What is the new position?	Lat 00°00′ Long 159°00′E	**3**
		Lat 00°00′ Long 159°00′W	**7**
		Lat 00°00′ Long 159°59′W	**8**

The second basic problem in navigation is to find the new position after sailing along a known True Course for a known Distance.

Finding the new position

Your present position is 63°09′S 98°31′W. You sail for 301 miles along a True Course of 031° (N31°E). What is the new position?

First, find the D.Lat and the Departure. You can do this by using the traverse table (page 482) or you can use the necessary formulae (page 945). The True Course is *N31°E*. So the D.Lat will be *N* and the Departure will be *E*:

    D.Lat   =258 miles N=258′N=4°18′N
    Departure=155 miles E

Next, find the new latitude:

    Lat (F)   63°09′S ⎫ You are sailing in a northerly direction in a southerly
    D.Lat   4°18′N ⎭ latitude. So your latitude becomes *less* southerly.
    Lat (T)   58°51′S

Now you have the two latitudes you can find the M.Lat:

    Lat (F)   63°09′S ⎫ Add the two latitudes and divide the result by 2. Direction
    Lat (T)   58°51′S ⎭ N or S is unimportant.
    M.Lat   61°00′

Now you have the M.Lat and the Departure, you can find the D.Long by using the traverse table (page 734) or by using the formula for converting Departure to D.Long (D.Long=Departure×sec (M.Lat)). The Departure is E and so the D.Long (320′=5°20′) will also be E. You can now find the new longitude:

    Long (F)   98°31′W ⎫ You are sailing in an easterly direction in a westerly
    D.Long   5°20′E ⎭ longitude. So your longitude will be *less* westerly.
    Long (T)   93°11′W

A ship sails from a position 27°23′N 160°34′E . . .

A.	It sails 388 miles on a True Course of 300°. Find the D.Lat and the Departure.	D.Lat=336′N Dep =194 miles W	**3**
		D.Lat=194′N Dep =336 miles W	**4**
		D.Lat=194′N Dep =336 miles E	**5**
B.	Now find the new latitude and the M.Lat.	Lat (T)=30°37′N M.Lat =29°00′	**2**
		Lat (T)=24°07′N M.Lat =29°00′	**6**
		Lat (T)=30°37′N M.Lat =58°00′	**7**
C.	Now find the D.Long and the new longitude.	D.Long =384′W Long (T)=154°10′E	**1**
		D.Long =384′E Long (T)=167°00′E	**8**
		D.Long =384′W Long (T)=154°10′W	**9**

Correct. Now read on.

When you navigate by calculation you have the choice of three methods. All three methods are based on these formulae, or on variants of these formulae:

Departure = D.Long × cos (M.Lat)

D.Long = Departure × sec (M.Lat)

$$\frac{\text{Departure}}{\text{D.Lat}} = \tan (\text{Course})$$

D.Lat = Distance × cos (Course)

Departure = Distance × sin (Course)

Navigation by 'Natural Functions of Angles' table
If you are prepared to multiply or divide figures containing three or more decimal places, all you need are the formulae above together with a table of the 'Natural Functions of Angles'.

Navigation by logarithmic tables
If you wish to reduce multiplication and division to addition and subtraction, all you need are the formulae above together with logarithmic tables (including 'Logs of Trig Functions').

Navigation by traverse table
If—like most navigators—you wish to avoid mathematics as far as possible, all you need is the traverse table. We have seen that Departure, D.Lat, True Course and Distance are related according to trigonometrical ratios (pages 241 and 452). The traverse table works out all these ratios for the navigator over distances up to 600 miles—the distance limit for *accurate* calculations when M.Lat (mean latitude) is used in place of middle latitude (page 629).

All the above tables can be found inside any established volume of navigation tables.

Choose the correct answer in each of these

A. You wish to navigate by calculation. You are prepared to multiply and divide. In addition to the formulae above, what will you need?

'Natural Functions of Angles' table **3**

Logarithmic tables **7**

Traverse table **8**

B. You wish to navigate by calculation. You are prepared to add and subtract but not to multiply and divide. In addition to the formulae above, what will you need?

Traverse table **1**

'Natural Functions of Angles' table **5**

Logarithmic tables **6**

C. You wish to navigate by calculation. You want to avoid mathematics as far as possible. What will you need to help you?

Traverse table **2**

'Natural Functions of Angles' table **4**

Logarithmic tables **9**

You have failed to grasp an important point.

You chose the wrong answer to all three questions in the last exercise—
and you made exactly the same mistake in each of them.

In each case you carried out your subtractions on a decimal base, forgetting
that there are only *sixty* minutes in one degree. Let's take a further example:

Long (F) 20°35′W ⎱ Since you are sailing from a Westerly longitude to a
Long (T) 18°45′W ⎰ *less* Westerly longitude, your D.Long is Easterly (E).

To find your D.Long you must subtract the smaller longitude from the larger
longitude. This means subtracting 45′ from 35′ and this, in turn, means
'borrowing' 1° and turning it into 60′. You now subtract 45′ from 95′ (35′+
60′):

D.Long=1°50′E or 110′E

Now tackle the repeat exercise below.

D.Long=distance E or W in minutes or degrees and minutes.

		110′E	**1**
	True Course: 090° (due E)		
A.	Long (F) 65°35′W	110′W	**8**
	Long (T) 63°45′W		
	What is the D.Long?	150′E	**9**
		526′E	**3**
	True Course: 270° (due W)		
B.	Long (F) 107°44′W	566′W	**4**
	Long (T) 116°30′W		
	What is the D.Long?	526′W	**5**
		320′E	**2**
	True Course: 270° (due W)		
C.	Long (F) 177°50′W	360′W	**6**
	Long (T) 176°50′E		
	What is the D.Long?	320′W	**7**

You have failed to grasp an important point.

You chose the wrong answer to questions A and B in the last exercise. And you made the same kind of mistake in each of them. In fact you have forgotten something explained earlier. Look at these rules carefully. There is no need to memorise them—they are simply a matter of common sense:

When you sail from a northerly latitude to a *less* northerly latitude your D.Lat will be southerly (S).

When you sail from a southerly latitude to a *less* southerly latitude your D.Lat will be northerly (N).

When you sail from an easterly longitude to a *less* easterly longitude your D.Long will be westerly (W).

When you sail from a westerly longitude to a *less* westerly longitude your D.Long will be easterly (E).

Get hold of an atlas—any atlas—and you will see that these rules make perfect sense.

Now tackle the repeat exercise below.

Some more practice with D.Lat, D.Long and M.Lat.

A. A ship sails between positions: 14°45′N 61°40′E (From) 11°55′N 57°50′E (To) What is the D.Lat?	210′S	**2**
	170′S	**4**
	170′N	**9**
B. What is the D.Long?	270′W	**3**
	230′E	**7**
	230′W	**8**
C. What is the M.Lat?	13°20′	**1**
	13°00′	**5**
	26°40′	**6**

The first basic problem in navigation is to find the Distance and True Course between two positions. We are now ready to tackle this.

Finding the True Course and Distance

You intend to sail from a position 27°35′N 45°42′W to a position 30°25′N 40°19′W. What is the Distance and True Course to steer?

First, find the D.Lat and D.Long:

Lat (F)	27°35′N		Long (F)	45°42′W
Lat (T)	30°25′N		Long (T)	40°19′W
D.Lat	2°50′N=170′N		D.Long	5°23′E=323′E

Next, find the M.Lat:

Lat (F)   27°35′N ⎫ Add the two latitudes and divide the result by 2. Direction
Lat (T)   30°25′N ⎰ N or S is unimportant.
M.Lat   29°00′

Now that you have the M.Lat and the D.Long, you can find the Departure by using the traverse table (page 734) or by using the formula for converting D.Long to Departure (Dep=D.Long×cos (M.Lat)). The D.Long is E and so the Departure (now in miles) will also be E:

Departure=282.5 miles E
D.Lat   =170 miles N (1′ D.Lat=1 mile)

Now that you have the D.Lat and the Departure, you can find the True Course and Distance by using the traverse table (page 482) or by using the formulae for finding Course and Distance (page 945). The D.Lat is *N* and the Departure is *E*. So:

Distance   =330 miles
True Course =N59°E=059°

A ship sails from 60°37′N 21°00′W to 57°23′N 24°37′W . . .

A.	Find the D.Lat, D.Long and M.Lat.	D.Lat=194′N D.Long=217′W M.Lat=59°00′		**3**
		D.Lat=194′S D.Long=217′E M.Lat=59°00′		**7**
		D.Lat=194′S D.Long=217′W M.Lat=59°00′		**8**
B.	Now find the Departure.	Departure=111.8 miles E		**2**
		Departure=186 miles W		**4**
		Departure=111.8 miles W		**9**
C.	Now find the True Course and Distance.	True Course=150° Distance=224 miles		**1**
		True Course=210° Distance=224 miles		**5**
		True Course=224° Distance=269 miles		**6**

Dist	D.Lat	Dep.	Dist	D.Lat	Dep.	Dist	D.Lat	Dep.	Dist	D.Lat	Dep.	Dist	D.Lat	Dep.
	D Lon	Dep.		D Lon	Dep.		D Lon	Dep.		D Lon	Dep.		D Lon	Dep.
1	00·9	00·5	61	53·4	29·6	121	105·8	58·7	181	158·3	87·8	241	210·8	116·8
2	01·7	01·0	62	54·2	30·1	122	106·7	59·1	182	159·2	88·2	242	211·7	117·3
3	02·6	01·5	63	55·1	30·5	123	107·6	59·6	183	160·1	88·7	243	212·5	117·8
4	03·5	01·9	64	56·0	31·0	124	108·5	60·1	184	160·9	89·2	244	213·4	118·3
5	04·4	02·4	65	56·9	31·5	125	109·3	60·6	185	161·8	89·7	245	214·3	118·8
6	05·2	02·9	66	57·7	32·0	126	110·2	61·1	186	162·7	90·2	246	215·2	119·3
7	06·1	03·4	67	58·6	32·5	127	111·1	61·6	187	163·6	90·7	247	216·0	119·7
8	07·0	03·9	68	59·5	33·0	128	112·0	62·1	188	164·4	91·1	248	216·9	120·2
9	07·9	04·4	69	60·3	33·5	129	112·8	62·5	189	165·3	91·6	249	217·8	120·7
10	08·7	04·8	70	61·2	33·9	130	113·7	63·0	190	166·2	92·1	250	218·7	121·2
11	09·6	05·3	71	62·1	34·4	131	114·6	63·5	191	167·1	92·6	251	219·5	121·7
12	10·5	05·8	72	63·0	34·9	132	115·4	64·0	192	167·9	93·1	252	220·4	122·2
13	11·4	06·3	73	63·8	35·4	133	116·3	64·5	193	168·8	93·6	253	221·3	122·7
14	12·2	06·8	74	64·7	35·9	134	117·2	65·0	194	169·7	94·1	254	222·2	123·1
15	13·1	07·3	75	65·6	36·4	135	118·1	65·4	195	170·6	94·5	255	223·0	123·6
16	14·0	07·8	76	66·5	36·8	136	118·9	65·9	196	171·4	95·0	256	223·9	124·1
17	14·9	08·2	77	67·3	37·3	137	119·8	66·4	197	172·3	95·5	257	224·8	124·6
18	15·7	08·7	78	68·2	37·8	138	120·7	66·9	198	173·2	96·0	258	225·7	125·1
19	16·6	09·2	79	69·1	38·3	139	121·6	67·4	199	174·0	96·5	259	226·5	125·6
20	17·5	09·7	80	70·0	38·8	140	122·4	67·9	200	174·9	97·0	260	227·4	126·1
21	18·4	10·2	81	70·8	39·3	141	123·3	68·4	201	175·8	97·4	261	228·3	126·5
22	19·2	10·7	82	71·7	39·8	142	124·2	68·8	202	176·7	97·9	262	229·2	127·0
23	20·1	11·2	83	72·6	40·2	143	125·1	69·3	203	177·5	98·4	263	230·0	127·5
24	21·0	11·6	84	73·5	40·7	144	125·9	69·8	204	178·4	98·9	264	230·9	128·0
25	21·9	12·1	85	74·3	41·2	145	126·8	70·3	205	179·3	99·4	265	231·8	128·5
26	22·7	12·6	86	75·2	41·7	146	127·7	70·8	206	180·2	99·9	266	232·6	129·0
27	23·6	13·1	87	76·1	42·2	147	128·6	71·3	207	181·0	100·4	267	233·5	129·4
28	24·5	13·6	88	77·0	42·7	148	129·4	71·8	208	181·9	100·8	268	234·4	129·9
29	25·4	14·1	89	77·8	43·1	149	130·3	72·2	209	182·8	101·3	269	235·3	130·4
30	26·2	14·5	90	78·7	43·6	150	131·2	72·7	210	183·7	101·8	270	236·1	130·9
31	27·1	15·0	91	79·6	44·1	151	132·1	73·2	211	184·5	102·3	271	237·0	131·4
32	28·0	15·5	92	80·5	44·6	152	132·9	73·7	212	185·4	102·8	272	237·9	131·9
33	28·9	16·0	93	81·3	45·1	153	133·8	74·2	213	186·3	103·3	273	238·8	132·4
34	29·7	16·5	94	82·2	45·6	154	134·7	74·7	214	187·2	103·7	274	239·6	132·8
35	30·6	17·0	95	83·1	46·1	155	135·6	75·1	215	188·0	104·2	275	240·5	133·3
36	31·5	17·5	96	84·0	46·5	156	136·4	75·6	216	188·9	104·7	276	241·4	133·8
37	32·4	17·9	97	84·8	47·0	157	137·3	76·1	217	189·8	105·2	277	242·3	134·3
38	33·2	18·4	98	85·7	47·5	158	138·2	76·6	218	190·7	105·7	278	243·1	134·8
39	34·1	18·9	99	86·6	48·0	159	139·1	77·1	219	191·5	106·2	279	244·0	135·3
40	35·0	19·4	100	87·5	48·5	160	139·9	77·6	220	192·4	106·7	280	244·9	135·7
41	35·9	19·9	101	88·3	49·0	161	140·8	78·1	221	193·3	107·1	281	245·8	136·2
42	36·7	20·4	102	89·2	49·5	162	141·7	78·5	222	194·2	107·6	282	246·6	136·7
43	37·6	20·8	103	90·1	49·9	163	142·6	79·0	223	195·0	108·1	283	247·5	137·2
44	38·5	21·3	104	91·0	50·4	164	143·4	79·5	224	195·9	108·6	284	248·4	137·7
45	39·4	21·8	105	91·8	50·9	165	144·3	80·0	225	196·8	109·1	285	249·3	138·2
46	40·2	22·3	106	92·7	51·4	166	145·2	80·5	226	197·7	109·6	286	250·1	138·7
47	41·1	22·8	107	93·6	51·9	167	146·1	81·0	227	198·5	110·1	287	251·0	139·1
48	42·0	23·3	108	94·5	52·4	168	146·9	81·4	228	199·4	110·5	288	251·9	139·6
49	42·9	23·8	109	95·3	52·8	169	147·8	81·9	229	200·3	111·0	289	252·8	140·1
50	43·7	24·2	110	96·2	53·3	170	148·7	82·4	230	201·2	111·5	290	253·6	140·6
51	44·6	24·7	111	97·1	53·8	171	149·6	82·9	231	202·0	112·0	291	254·5	141·1
52	45·5	25·2	112	98·0	54·3	172	150·4	83·4	232	202·9	112·5	292	255·4	141·6
53	46·4	25·7	113	98·8	54·8	173	151·3	83·9	233	203·8	113·0	293	256·3	142·0
54	47·2	26·2	114	99·7	55·3	174	152·2	84·4	234	204·7	113·4	294	257·1	142·5
55	48·1	26·7	115	100·6	55·8	175	153·1	84·8	235	205·5	113·9	295	258·0	143·0
56	49·0	27·1	116	101·5	56·2	176	153·9	85·3	236	206·4	114·4	296	258·9	143·5
57	49·9	27·6	117	102·3	56·7	177	154·8	85·8	237	207·3	114·9	297	259·8	144·0
58	50·7	28·1	118	103·2	57·2	178	155·7	86·3	238	208·2	115·4	298	260·6	144·5
59	51·6	28·6	119	104·1	57·7	179	156·6	86·8	239	209·0	115·9	299	261·5	145·0
60	52·5	29·1	120	105·0	58·2	180	157·4	87·3	240	209·9	116·4	300	262·4	145·4
Dist	Dep.	D.Lat	Dist	Dep.	D.Lat	Dist	Dep.	D.Lat	Dist	Dep.	D.Lat	Dist	Dep.	D.Lat
D Lon		Dep.	D Lon		Dep.	D Lon		Dep.	D Lon		Dep.	D Lon		Dep.

DLon Dep.			DLon Dep.			DLon Dep.			DLon Dep.			DLon Dep.		
Dist	D.Lat	Dep.	Dist	D.Lat	Dep.	Dist	D.Lat	Dep.	Dist	D.Lat	Dep.	Dist	D.Lat	Dep.
301	263·3	145·9	361	315·7	175·0	421	368·2	204·1	481	420·7	233·2	541	473·2	262·3
302	264·1	146·4	362	316·6	175·5	422	369·1	204·6	482	421·6	233·7	542	474·0	262·8
303	265·0	146·9	363	317·5	176·0	423	370·0	205·1	483	422·4	234·2	543	474·9	263·3
304	265·9	147·4	364	318·4	176·5	424	370·8	205·6	484	423·3	234·6	544	475·8	263·7
305	266·8	147·9	365	319·2	177·0	425	371·7	206·0	485	424·2	235·1	545	476·7	264·2
306	267·6	148·4	366	320·1	177·4	426	372·6	206·5	486	425·1	235·6	546	477·5	264·7
307	268·5	148·8	367	321·0	177·9	427	373·5	207·0	487	425·9	236·1	547	478·4	265·2
308	269·4	149·3	368	321·9	178·4	428	374·3	207·5	488	426·8	236·6	548	479·3	265·7
309	270·3	149·8	369	322·7	178·9	429	375·2	208·0	489	427·7	237·1	549	480·2	266·2
310	271·1	150·3	370	323·6	179·4	430	376·1	208·5	490	428·6	237·6	550	481·0	266·6
311	272·0	150·8	371	324·5	179·9	431	377·0	209·0	491	429·4	238·0	551	481·9	267·1
312	272·9	151·3	372	325·4	180·3	432	377·8	209·4	492	430·3	238·5	552	482·8	267·6
313	273·8	151·7	373	326·2	180·8	433	378·7	209·9	493	431·2	239·0	553	483·7	268·1
314	274·6	152·2	374	327·1	181·3	434	379·6	210·4	494	432·1	239·5	554	484·5	268·6
315	275·5	152·7	375	328·0	181·8	435	380·5	210·9	495	432·9	240·0	555	485·4	269·1
316	276·4	153·2	376	328·9	182·3	436	381·3	211·4	496	433·8	240·5	556	486·3	269·6
317	277·3	153·7	377	329·7	182·8	437	382·2	211·9	497	434·7	241·0	557	487·2	270·0
318	278·1	154·2	378	330·6	183·3	438	383·1	212·3	498	435·6	241·4	558	488·0	270·5
319	279·0	154·7	379	331·5	183·7	439	384·0	212·8	499	436·4	241·9	559	488·9	271·0
320	279·9	155·1	380	332·4	184·2	440	384·8	213·3	500	437·3	242·4	560	489·8	271·5
321	280·8	155·6	381	333·2	184·7	441	385·7	213·8	501	438·2	242·9	561	490·7	272·0
322	281·6	156·1	382	334·1	185·2	442	386·6	214·3	502	439·1	243·4	562	491·5	272·5
323	282·5	156·6	383	335·0	185·7	443	387·5	214·8	503	439·9	243·9	563	492·4	272·9
324	283·4	157·1	384	335·9	186·2	444	388·3	215·3	504	440·8	244·3	564	493·3	273·4
325	284·3	157·6	385	336·7	186·7	445	389·2	215·7	505	441·7	244·8	565	494·2	273·9
326	285·1	158·0	386	337·6	187·1	446	390·1	216·2	506	442·6	245·3	566	495·0	274·4
327	286·0	158·5	387	338·5	187·6	447	391·0	216·7	507	443·4	245·8	567	495·9	274·9
328	286·9	159·0	388	339·4	188·1	448	391·8	217·2	508	444·3	246·3	568	496·8	275·4
329	287·7	159·5	389	340·2	188·6	449	392·7	217·7	509	445·2	246·8	569	497·7	275·9
330	288·6	160·0	390	341·1	189·1	450	393·6	218·2	510	446·1	247·3	570	498·5	276·3
331	289·5	160·5	391	342·0	189·6	451	394·5	218·6	511	446·9	247·7	571	499·4	276·8
332	290·4	161·0	392	342·9	190·0	452	395·3	219·1	512	447·8	248·2	572	500·3	277·3
333	291·2	161·4	393	343·7	190·5	453	396·2	219·6	513	448·7	248·7	573	501·2	277·8
334	292·1	161·9	394	344·6	191·0	454	397·1	220·1	514	449·6	249·2	574	502·0	278·3
335	293·0	162·4	395	345·5	191·5	455	398·0	220·6	515	450·4	249·7	575	502·9	278·8
336	293·9	162·9	396	346·3	192·0	456	398·8	221·1	516	451·3	250·2	576	503·8	279·3
337	294·7	163·4	397	347·2	192·5	457	399·7	221·6	517	452·2	250·6	577	504·7	279·7
338	295·6	163·9	398	348·1	193·0	458	400·6	222·0	518	453·1	251·1	578	505·5	280·2
339	296·5	164·4	399	349·0	193·4	459	401·5	222·5	519	453·9	251·6	579	506·4	280·7
340	297·4	164·8	400	349·8	193·9	460	402·3	223·0	520	454·8	252·1	580	507·3	281·2
341	298·2	165·3	401	350·7	194·4	461	403·2	223·5	521	455·7	252·6	581	508·2	281·7
342	299·1	165·8	402	351·6	194·9	462	404·1	224·0	522	456·6	253·1	582	509·0	282·2
343	300·0	166·3	403	352·5	195·4	463	404·9	224·5	523	457·4	253·6	583	509·9	282·6
344	300·9	166·8	404	353·3	195·9	464	405·8	225·0	524	458·3	254·0	584	510·7	283·1
345	301·7	167·3	405	354·2	196·3	465	406·7	225·4	525	459·2	254·5	585	511·7	283·6
346	302·6	167·7	406	355·1	196·8	466	407·6	225·9	526	460·0	255·0	586	512·5	284·1
347	303·5	168·2	407	356·0	197·3	467	408·4	226·4	527	460·9	255·5	587	513·4	284·6
348	304·4	168·7	408	356·8	197·8	468	409·3	226·9	528	461·8	256·0	588	514·3	285·1
349	305·2	169·2	409	357·7	198·3	469	410·2	227·4	529	462·7	256·5	589	515·2	285·6
350	306·1	169·7	410	358·6	198·8	470	411·1	227·9	530	463·5	256·9	590	516·0	286·0
351	307·0	170·2	411	359·5	199·3	471	411·9	228·3	531	464·4	257·4	591	516·9	286·5
352	307·9	170·7	412	360·3	199·7	472	412·8	228·8	532	465·3	257·9	592	517·8	287·0
353	308·7	171·1	413	361·2	200·2	473	413·7	229·3	533	466·2	258·4	593	518·6	287·5
354	309·6	171·6	414	362·1	200·7	474	414·6	229·8	534	467·0	258·9	594	519·5	288·0
355	310·5	172·1	415	363·0	201·2	475	415·4	230·3	535	467·9	259·4	595	520·4	288·5
356	311·4	172·6	416	363·8	201·7	476	416·3	230·8	536	468·8	259·9	596	521·3	288·9
357	312·2	173·1	417	364·7	202·2	477	417·2	231·3	537	469·6	260·3	597	522·2	289·4
358	313·1	173·6	418	365·6	202·7	478	418·1	231·7	538	470·5	260·8	598	523·0	289·9
359	314·0	174·0	419	366·5	203·1	479	418·9	232·2	539	471·4	261·3	599	523·9	290·4
360	314·9	174·5	420	367·3	203·6	480	419·8	232·7	540	472·3	261·8	600	524·8	290·9
Dist	Dep.	D.Lat	Dist	Dep.	D.Lat	Dist	Dep.	D.Lat	Dist	Dep.	D.Lat	Dist	Dep.	D.Lat
DLon		Dep.	DLon		Dep.	DLon		Dep.	DLon		Dep.	DLon		Dep.

30°

330° ↑
210°

TRAVERSE TABLE
30 DEGREES.

↑030°
150°

2h 0m

Dist	D. Lat	Dep.	Dist	D. Lat	Dep.	Dist	D. Lat	Dep.	Dist	D. Lat	Dep.	Dist	D. Lat	Dep.
D Lon	Dep.		D Lon	Dep.		D Lon	Dep.		D Lon	Dep.		D Lon	Dep.	
1	00·9	00·5	61	52·8	30·5	121	104·8	60·5	181	156·8	90·5	241	208·7	120·5
2	01·7	01·0	62	53·7	31·0	122	105·7	61·0	182	157·6	91·0	242	209·6	121·0
3	02·6	01·5	63	54·6	31·5	123	106·5	61·5	183	158·5	91·5	243	210·4	121·5
4	03·5	02·0	64	55·4	32·0	124	107·4	62·0	184	159·3	92·0	244	211·3	122·0
5	04·3	02·5	65	56·3	32·5	125	108·3	62·5	185	160·2	92·5	245	212·2	122·5
6	05·2	03·0	66	57·2	33·0	126	109·1	63·0	186	161·1	93·0	246	213·0	123·0
7	06·1	03·5	67	58·0	33·5	127	110·0	63·5	187	161·9	93·5	247	213·9	123·5
8	06·9	04·0	68	58·9	34·0	128	110·9	64·0	188	162·8	94·0	248	214·8	124·0
9	07·8	04·5	69	59·8	34·5	129	111·7	64·5	189	163·7	94·5	249	215·6	124·5
10	08·7	05·0	70	60·6	35·0	130	112·6	65·0	190	164·5	95·0	250	216·5	125·0
11	09·5	05·5	71	61·5	35·5	131	113·4	65·5	191	165·4	95·5	251	217·4	125·5
12	10·4	06·0	72	62·4	36·0	132	114·3	66·0	192	166·3	96·0	252	218·2	126·0
13	11·3	06·5	73	63·2	36·5	133	115·2	66·5	193	167·1	96·5	253	219·1	126·5
14	12·1	07·0	74	64·1	37·0	134	116·0	67·0	194	168·0	97·0	254	220·0	127·0
15	13·0	07·5	75	65·0	37·5	135	116·9	67·5	195	168·9	97·5	255	220·8	127·5
16	13·9	08·0	76	65·8	38·0	136	117·8	68·0	196	169·7	98·0	256	221·7	128·0
17	14·7	08·5	77	66·7	38·5	137	118·6	68·5	197	170·6	98·5	257	222·6	128·5
18	15·6	09·0	78	67·5	39·0	138	119·5	69·0	198	171·5	99·0	258	223·4	129·0
19	16·5	09·5	79	68·4	39·5	139	120·4	69·5	199	172·3	99·5	259	224·3	129·5
20	17·3	10·0	80	69·3	40·0	140	121·2	70·0	200	173·2	100·0	260	225·2	130·0
21	18·2	10·5	81	70·1	40·5	141	122·1	70·5	201	174·1	100·5	261	226·0	130·5
22	19·1	11·0	82	71·0	41·0	142	123·0	71·0	202	174·9	101·0	262	226·9	131·0
23	19·9	11·5	83	71·9	41·5	143	123·8	71·5	203	175·8	101·5	263	227·8	131·5
24	20·8	12·0	84	72·7	42·0	144	124·7	72·0	204	176·7	102·0	264	228·6	132·0
25	21·7	12·5	85	73·6	42·5	145	125·6	72·5	205	177·5	102·5	265	229·5	132·5
26	22·5	13·0	86	74·5	43·0	146	126·4	73·0	206	178·4	103·0	266	230·4	133·0
27	23·4	13·5	87	75·3	43·5	147	127·3	73·5	207	179·3	103·5	267	231·2	133·5
28	24·2	14·0	88	76·2	44·0	148	128·2	74·0	208	180·1	104·0	268	232·1	134·0
29	25·1	14·5	89	77·1	44·5	149	129·0	74·5	209	181·0	104·5	269	233·0	134·5
30	26·0	15·0	90	77·9	45·0	150	129·9	75·0	210	181·9	105·0	270	233·8	135·0
31	26·8	15·5	91	78·8	45·5	151	130·8	75·5	211	182·7	105·5	271	234·7	135·5
32	27·7	16·0	92	79·7	46·0	152	131·6	76·0	212	183·6	106·0	272	235·6	136·0
33	28·6	16·5	93	80·5	46·5	153	132·5	76·5	213	184·5	106·5	273	236·4	136·5
34	29·4	17·0	94	81·4	47·0	154	133·4	77·0	214	185·3	107·0	274	237·3	137·0
35	30·3	17·5	95	82·3	47·5	155	134·2	77·5	215	186·2	107·5	275	238·2	137·5
36	31·2	18·0	96	83·1	48·0	156	135·1	78·0	216	187·1	108·0	276	239·0	138·0
37	32·0	18·5	97	84·0	48·5	157	136·0	78·5	217	187·9	108·5	277	239·9	138·5
38	32·9	19·0	98	84·9	49·0	158	136·8	79·0	218	188·8	109·0	278	240·8	139·0
39	33·8	19·5	99	85·7	49·5	159	137·7	79·5	219	189·7	109·5	279	241·6	139·5
40	34·6	20·0	100	86·6	50·0	160	138·6	80·0	220	190·5	110·0	280	242·5	140·0
41	35·5	20·5	101	87·5	50·5	161	139·4	80·5	221	191·4	110·5	281	243·4	140·5
42	36·4	21·0	102	88·3	51·0	162	140·3	81·0	222	192·3	111·0	282	244·2	141·0
43	37·2	21·5	103	89·2	51·5	163	141·2	81·5	223	193·1	111·5	283	245·1	141·5
44	38·1	22·0	104	90·1	52·0	164	142·0	82·0	224	194·0	112·0	284	246·0	142·0
45	39·0	22·5	105	90·9	52·5	165	142·9	82·5	225	194·9	112·5	285	246·8	142·5
46	39·8	23·0	106	91·8	53·0	166	143·8	83·0	226	195·7	113·0	286	247·7	143·0
47	40·7	23·5	107	92·7	53·5	167	144·6	83·5	227	196·6	113·5	287	248·5	143·5
48	41·6	24·0	108	93·5	54·0	168	145·5	84·0	228	197·5	114·0	288	249·4	144·0
49	42·4	24·5	109	94·4	54·5	169	146·4	84·5	229	198·3	114·5	289	250·3	144·5
50	43·3	25·0	110	95·3	55·0	170	147·2	85·0	230	199·2	115·0	290	251·1	145·0
51	44·2	25·5	111	96·1	55·5	171	148·1	85·5	231	200·1	115·5	291	252·0	145·5
52	45·0	26·0	112	97·0	56·0	172	149·0	86·0	232	200·9	116·0	292	252·9	146·0
53	45·9	26·5	113	97·9	56·5	173	149·8	86·5	233	201·8	116·5	293	253·7	146·5
54	46·8	27·0	114	98·7	57·0	174	150·7	87·0	234	202·6	117·0	294	254·6	147·0
55	47·6	27·5	115	99·6	57·5	175	151·6	87·5	235	203·5	117·5	295	255·5	147·5
56	48·5	28·0	116	100·5	58·0	176	152·4	88·0	236	204·4	118·0	296	256·3	148·0
57	49·4	28·5	117	101·3	58·5	177	153·3	88·5	237	205·2	118·5	297	257·2	148·5
58	50·2	29·0	118	102·2	59·0	178	154·2	89·0	238	206·1	119·0	298	258·1	149·0
59	51·1	29·5	119	103·1	59·5	179	155·0	89·5	239	207·0	119·5	299	258·9	149·5
60	52·0	30·0	120	103·9	60·0	180	155·9	90·0	240	207·8	120·0	300	259·8	150·0
Dist	Dep.	D. Lat	Dist	Dep.	D. Lat	Dist	Dep.	D. Lat	Dist	Dep.	D. Lat	Dist	Dep.	D. Lat
D Lon		Dep.	D Lon		Dep.	D Lon		Dep.	D Lon		Dep.	D Lon		Dep.

60°

300° ↑
240°

60 DEGREES.

↑060
120

4h 0m

D Lon / Dep.			D Lon / Dep.			D Lon / Dep.			D Lon / Dep.			D Lon / Dep.		
Dist	D. Lat	Dep.	Dist	D. Lat	Dep.	Dist	D. Lat	Dep.	Dist	D. Lat	Dep.	Dist	D. Lat	Dep.
301	260·7	150·5	361	312·6	180·5	421	364·6	210·5	481	416·6	240·5	541	468·5	270·5
302	261·5	151·0	362	313·5	181·0	422	365·5	211·0	482	417·4	241·0	542	469·4	271·0
303	262·4	151·5	363	314·4	181·5	423	366·3	211·5	483	418·3	241·5	543	470·3	271·5
304	263·3	152·0	364	315·2	182·0	424	367·2	212·0	484	419·2	242·0	544	471 1	272·0
305	264·1	152·5	365	316·1	182·5	425	368·1	212·5	485	420·0	242·5	545	472·0	272·5
306	265·0	153·0	366	317·0	183·0	426	368·9	213·0	486	420·9	243·0	546	472·8	273·0
307	265·9	153·5	367	317·8	183·5	427	369·8	213·5	487	421·8	243·5	547	473·7	273·5
308	266·7	154·0	368	318·7	184·0	428	370·7	214·0	488	422·6	244·0	548	474·6	274·0
309	267·6	154·5	369	319·6	184·5	429	371·5	214·5	489	423·5	244·5	549	475·4	274·5
310	268·5	155·0	370	320·4	185·0	430	372·4	215·0	490	424·4	245·0	550	476·3	275·0
311	269·3	155·5	371	321·3	185·5	431	373·3	215·5	491	425·2	245·5	551	477·2	275·5
312	270·2	156·0	372	322·2	186·0	432	374·1	216·0	492	426·1	246·0	552	478·0	276·0
313	271·1	156·5	373	323·0	186·5	433	375·0	216·5	493	427·0	246·5	553	478·9	276·5
314	271·9	157·0	374	323·9	187·0	434	375·9	217·0	494	427·8	247·0	554	479·8	277·0
315	272·8	157·5	375	324·8	187·5	435	376·7	217·5	495	428·7	247·5	555	480·6	277·5
316	273·7	158·0	376	325·6	188·0	436	377·6	218·0	496	429·5	248·0	556	481·5	278·0
317	274·5	158·5	377	326·5	188·5	437	378·5	218·5	497	430·4	248·5	557	482·4	278·5
318	275·4	159·0	378	327·4	189·0	438	379·3	219·0	498	431·3	249·0	558	483·2	279·0
319	276·3	159·5	379	328·2	189·5	439	380·2	219·5	499	432·1	249·5	559	484·1	279·5
320	277·1	160·0	380	329·1	190·0	440	381·1	220·0	500	433·0	250·0	560	485·0	280·0
321	278·0	160·5	381	330·0	190·5	441	381·9	220·5	501	433·9	250·5	561	485·8	280·5
322	278·9	161·0	382	330·8	191·0	442	382·8	221·0	502	434·7	251·0	562	486·7	281·0
323	279·7	161·5	383	331·7	191·5	443	383·6	221·5	503	435·6	251·5	563	487·6	281·5
324	280·6	162·0	384	332·6	192·0	444	384·5	222·0	504	436·5	252·0	564	488·4	282·0
325	281·5	162·5	385	333·4	192·5	445	385·4	222·5	505	437·3	252·5	565	489·3	282·5
326	282·3	163·0	386	334·3	193·0	446	386·3	223·0	506	438·2	253·0	566	490·2	283·0
327	283·2	163·5	387	335·2	193·5	447	387·1	223·5	507	439·1	253·5	567	491·0	283·5
328	284·1	164·0	388	336·0	194·0	448	388·0	224·0	508	439·9	254·0	568	491·9	284·0
329	284·9	164·5	389	336·9	194·5	449	388·8	224·5	509	440·8	254·5	569	492·8	284·5
330	285·8	165·0	390	337·7	195·0	450	389 7	225·0	510	441 7	255·0	570	493·6	285·0
331	286·7	165·5	391	338·6	195·5	451	390·6	225·5	511	442·5	255·5	571	494·5	285·5
332	287·5	166·0	392	339·5	196·0	452	391·4	226·0	512	443·4	256·0	572	495·4	286·0
333	288·4	166·5	393	340·3	196·5	453	392·3	226·5	513	444·3	256·5	573	496·2	286·5
334	289·3	167·0	394	341·2	197·0	454	393·2	227·0	514	445·1	257·0	574	497·1	287·0
335	290·1	167·5	395	342·1	197·5	455	394·0	227·5	515	446·0	257·5	575	498·0	287·5
336	291·0	168·0	396	342·9	198·0	456	394·9	228·0	516	446·9	258·0	576	498·8	288·0
337	291·9	168·5	397	343·8	198·5	457	395·8	228·5	517	447·7	258·5	577	499·7	288·5
338	292·7	169·0	398	344·7	199·0	458	396·6	229·0	518	448·6	259·0	578	500·6	289·0
339	293·6	169·5	399	345·5	199·5	459	397·5	229·5	519	449·5	259·5	579	501·3	289·5
340	294·5	170·0	400	346·4	200·0	460	398·4	230·0	520	450·3	260·0	580	502·3	290·0
341	295·3	170·5	401	347·3	200·5	461	399·2	230·5	521	451·2	260·5	581	503·2	290·5
342	296·2	171·0	402	348·1	201·0	462	400·1	231·0	522	452·1	261·0	582	504·0	291·0
343	297·0	171·5	403	349·0	201·5	463	401·0	231·5	523	452·9	261·5	583	504·9	291·5
344	297·9	172·0	404	349·9	202·0	464	401·8	232·0	524	453·8	262·0	584	505·8	292·0
345	298·8	172·5	405	350·7	202·5	465	402·7	232·5	525	454·7	262·5	585	506·6	292·5
346	299·6	173·0	406	351·6	203·0	466	403·6	233·0	526	455·5	263·0	586	507·5	293·0
347	300·5	173·5	407	352·5	203·5	467	404·4	233·5	527	456·4	263·5	587	508·4	293·5
348	301·4	174·0	408	353·3	204·0	468	405·3	234·0	528	457·3	264·0	588	509·2	294·0
349	302·2	174·5	409	354·2	204·5	469	406·2	234·5	529	458·1	264·5	589	510·1	294·5
350	303·1	175·0	410	355·1	205·0	470	407·0	235·0	530	459·0	265·0	590	511·0	295·0
351	304·0	175·5	411	355·9	205·5	471	407·9	235·5	531	459·9	265·5	591	511·8	295·5
352	304·8	176·0	412	356·8	206·0	472	408·8	236·0	532	460·7	266·0	592	512·7	296·0
353	305·7	176·5	413	357·7	206·5	473	409·6	236·5	533	461·6	266·5	593	513·6	296·5
354	306·6	177·0	414	358·5	207·0	474	410·5	237·0	534	462·5	267·0	594	514·4	297·0
355	307·4	177·5	415	359·4	207·5	475	411·4	237·5	535	463·3	267·5	595	515·3	297·5
356	308·3	178·0	416	360·3	208·0	476	412·2	238·0	536	464·2	268·0	596	516·2	298·0
357	309·2	178·5	417	361·1	208·5	477	413·1	238·5	537	465·1	268·5	597	517·0	298·5
358	310·0	179·0	418	362·0	209·0	478	414·0	239·0	538	465·9	269·0	598	517·9	299·0
359	310·9	179·5	419	362·9	209·5	479	414·8	239·5	539	466·8	269·5	599	518·7	299·5
360	311·8	180·0	420	363·7	210·0	480	415·7	240·0	540	467·7	270·0	600	519·6	300·0
Dist	Dep.	D. Lat	Dist	Dep.	D. Lat	Dist	Dep.	D. Lat	Dist	Dep.	D. Lat	Dist	Dep.	D. Lat
Lon		Dep.	D Lon		Dep.	D Lon		Dep.	D Lon		Dep.	D Lon		Dep.

D Lon / Dep.			D Lon / Dep.			D Lon / Dep.			D Lon / Dep.			D Lon / Dep.		
Dist	D.Lat	Dep.	Dist	D.Lat	Dep.	Dist	D.Lat	Dep.	Dist	D.Lat	Dep.	Dist	D.Lat	Dep.
1	00.9	00.5	61	52.3	31.4	121	103.7	62.3	181	155.1	93.2	241	206.6	124.1
2	01.7	01.0	62	53.1	31.9	122	104.6	62.8	182	156.0	93.7	242	207.4	124.6
3	02.6	01.5	63	54.0	32.4	123	105.4	63.3	183	156.9	94.3	243	208.3	125.2
4	03.4	02.1	64	54.9	33.0	124	106.3	63.9	184	157.7	94.8	244	209.1	125.7
5	04.3	02.6	65	55.7	33.5	125	107.1	64.4	185	158.6	95.3	245	210.0	126.2
6	05.1	03.1	66	56.6	34.0	126	108.0	64.9	186	159.4	95.8	246	210.9	126.7
7	06.0	03.6	67	57.4	34.5	127	108.9	65.4	187	160.3	96.3	247	211.7	127.2
8	06.9	04.1	68	58.3	35.0	128	109.7	65.9	188	161.1	96.8	248	212.6	127.7
9	07.7	04.6	69	59.1	35.5	129	110.6	66.4	189	162.0	97.3	249	213.4	128.2
10	08.6	05.2	70	60.0	36.1	130	111.4	67.0	190	162.9	97.9	250	214.3	128.8
11	09.4	05.7	71	60.9	36.6	131	112.3	67.5	191	163.7	98.4	251	215.1	129.3
12	10.3	06.2	72	61.7	37.1	132	113.1	68.0	192	164.6	98.9	252	216.0	129.8
13	11.1	06.7	73	62.6	37.6	133	114.0	68.5	193	165.4	99.4	253	216.9	130.3
14	12.0	07.2	74	63.4	38.1	134	114.9	69.0	194	166.3	99.9	254	217.7	130.8
15	12.9	07.7	75	64.3	38.6	135	115.7	69.5	195	167.1	100.4	255	218.6	131.3
16	13.7	08.2	76	65.1	39.1	136	116.6	70.0	196	168.0	100.9	256	219.4	131.8
17	14.6	08.8	77	66.0	39.7	137	117.4	70.6	197	168.9	101.5	257	220.3	132.4
18	15.4	09.3	78	66.9	40.2	138	118.3	71.1	198	169.7	102.0	258	221.1	132.9
19	16.3	09.8	79	67.7	40.7	139	119.1	71.6	199	170.6	102.5	259	222.0	133.4
20	17.1	10.3	80	68.6	41.2	140	120.0	72.1	200	171.4	103.0	260	222.9	133.9
21	18.0	10.8	81	69.4	41.7	141	120.9	72.6	201	172.3	103.5	261	223.7	134.4
22	18.9	11.3	82	70.3	42.2	142	121.7	73.1	202	173.1	104.0	262	224.6	134.9
23	19.7	11.8	83	71.1	42.7	143	122.6	73.7	203	174.0	104.6	263	225.4	135.5
24	20.6	12.4	84	72.0	43.3	144	123.4	74.2	204	174.9	105.1	264	226.3	136.0
25	21.4	12.9	85	72.9	43.8	145	124.3	74.7	205	175.7	105.6	265	227.1	136.5
26	22.3	13.4	86	73.7	44.3	146	125.1	75.2	206	176.6	106.1	266	228.0	137.0
27	23.1	13.9	87	74.6	44.8	147	126.0	75.7	207	177.4	106.6	267	228.9	137.5
28	24.0	14.4	88	75.4	45.3	148	126.9	76.2	208	178.3	107.1	268	229.7	138.0
29	24.9	14.9	89	76.3	45.8	149	127.7	76.7	209	179.1	107.6	269	230.6	138.5
30	25.7	15.5	90	77.1	46.4	150	128.6	77.3	210	180.0	108.2	270	231.4	139.1
31	26.6	16.0	91	78.0	46.9	151	129.4	77.8	211	180.9	108.7	271	232.3	139.6
32	27.4	16.5	92	78.9	47.4	152	130.3	78.3	212	181.7	109.2	272	233.1	140.1
33	28.3	17.0	93	79.7	47.9	153	131.1	78.8	213	182.6	109.7	273	234.0	140.6
34	29.1	17.5	94	80.6	48.4	154	132.0	79.3	214	183.4	110.2	274	234.9	141.1
35	30.0	18.0	95	81.4	48.9	155	132.9	79.8	215	184.3	110.7	275	235.7	141.6
36	30.9	18.5	96	82.3	49.4	156	133.7	80.3	216	185.1	111.2	276	236.6	142.2
37	31.7	19.1	97	83.1	50.0	157	134.6	80.9	217	186.0	111.8	277	237.4	142.7
38	32.6	19.6	98	84.0	50.5	158	135.4	81.4	218	186.9	112.3	278	238.3	143.2
39	33.4	20.1	99	84.9	51.0	159	136.3	81.9	219	187.7	112.8	279	239.1	143.7
40	34.3	20.6	100	85.7	51.5	160	137.1	82.4	220	188.6	113.3	280	240.0	144.2
41	35.1	21.1	101	86.6	52.0	161	138.0	82.9	221	189.4	113.8	281	240.9	144.7
42	36.0	21.6	102	87.4	52.5	162	138.9	83.4	222	190.3	114.3	282	241.7	145.2
43	36.9	22.1	103	88.3	53.0	163	139.7	84.0	223	191.1	114.9	283	242.6	145.8
44	37.7	22.7	104	89.1	53.6	164	140.6	84.5	224	192.0	115.4	284	243.4	146.3
45	38.6	23.2	105	90.0	54.1	165	141.4	85.0	225	192.9	115.9	285	244.3	146.8
46	39.4	23.7	106	90.9	54.6	166	142.3	85.5	226	193.7	116.4	286	245.1	147.3
47	40.3	24.2	107	91.7	55.1	167	143.1	86.0	227	194.6	116.9	287	246.0	147.8
48	41.1	24.7	108	92.6	55.6	168	144.0	86.5	228	195.4	117.4	288	246.9	148.3
49	42.0	25.2	109	93.4	56.1	169	144.9	87.0	229	196.3	117.9	289	247.7	148.8
50	42.9	25.8	110	94.3	56.7	170	145.7	87.6	230	197.1	118.5	290	248.6	149.4
51	43.7	26.3	111	95.1	57.2	171	146.6	88.1	231	198.0	119.0	291	249.4	149.9
52	44.6	26.8	112	96.0	57.7	172	147.4	88.6	232	198.9	119.5	292	250.3	150.4
53	45.4	27.3	113	96.9	58.2	173	148.3	89.1	233	199.7	120.0	293	251.2	150.9
54	46.3	27.8	114	97.7	58.7	174	149.1	89.6	234	200.6	120.5	294	252.0	151.4
55	47.1	28.3	115	98.6	59.2	175	150.0	90.1	235	201.4	121.0	295	252.9	151.9
56	48.0	28.8	116	99.4	59.7	176	150.9	90.6	236	202.3	121.5	296	253.7	152.5
57	48.9	29.4	117	100.3	60.3	177	151.7	91.2	237	203.1	122.1	297	254.6	153.0
58	49.7	29.9	118	101.1	60.8	178	152.6	91.7	238	204.0	122.6	298	255.4	153.5
59	50.6	30.4	119	102.0	61.3	179	153.4	92.2	239	204.9	123.1	299	256.3	154.0
60	51.4	30.9	120	102.9	61.8	180	154.3	92.7	240	205.7	123.6	300	257.1	154.5
Dist	Dep.	D.Lat	Dist	Dep.	D.Lat	Dist	Dep.	D.Lat	Dist	Dep.	D.Lat	Dist	Dep.	D.Lat
D Lon		Dep.	D Lon		Dep.	D Lon		Dep.	D Lon		Dep.	D Lon		Dep.

TRAVERSE TABLE
31 DEGREES.

D Lon	Dep.		D Lon	Dep.		D Lon	Dep.		D Lon	Dep.		D Lon	Dep.	
Dist	D.Lat	Dep.	Dist	D.Lat	Dep.	Dist	D.Lat	Dep.	Dist	D.Lat	Dep.	Dist	D.Lat	Dep.
301	258·0	155·0	361	309·4	185·9	421	360·9	216·8	481	412·3	247·7	541	463·7	278·6
302	258·9	155·5	362	310·3	186·4	422	361·7	217·3	482	413·2	248·2	542	464·6	279·2
303	259·7	156·1	363	311·2	187·0	423	362·6	217·9	483	414·0	248·8	543	465·4	279·7
304	260·6	156·6	364	312·0	187·5	424	363·4	218·4	484	414·9	249·3	544	466·3	280·2
305	261·4	157·1	365	312·9	188·0	425	364·3	218·9	485	415·7	249·8	545	467·2	280·7
306	262·3	157·6	366	313·7	188·5	426	365·2	219·4	486	416·6	250·3	546	468·0	281·2
307	263·2	158·1	367	314·6	189·0	427	366·0	219·9	487	417·4	250·8	547	468·9	281·7
308	264·0	158·6	368	315·4	189·5	428	366·9	220·4	488	418·3	251·3	548	469·7	282·2
309	264·9	159·1	369	316·3	190·0	429	367·7	221·0	489	419·2	251·9	549	470·6	282·8
310	265·7	159·7	370	317·2	190·6	430	368·6	221·5	490	420·0	252·4	550	471·5	283·3
311	266·6	160·2	371	318·0	191·1	431	369·4	222·0	491	420·9	252·9	551	472·3	283·8
312	267·4	160·7	372	318·9	191·6	432	370·3	222·5	492	421·7	253·4	552	473·2	284·3
313	268·3	161·2	373	319·7	192·1	433	371·2	223·0	493	422·6	253·9	553	474·0	284·8
314	269·2	161·7	374	320·6	192·6	434	372·0	223·5	494	423·4	254·4	554	474·9	285·3
315	270·0	162·2	375	321·4	193·1	435	372·9	224·0	495	424·3	254·9	555	475·7	285·8
316	270·9	162·8	376	322·3	193·7	436	373·7	224·6	496	425·2	255·5	556	476·6	286·4
317	271·7	163·3	377	323·2	194·2	437	374·6	225·1	497	426·0	256·0	557	477·4	286·9
318	272·6	163·8	378	324·0	194·7	438	375·4	225·6	498	426·9	256·5	558	478·3	287·4
319	273·4	164·3	379	324·9	195·2	439	376·3	226·1	499	427·7	257·0	559	479·2	287·9
320	274·3	164·8	380	325·7	195·7	440	377·2	226·6	500	428·6	257·5	560	480·0	288·4
321	275·2	165·3	381	326·6	196·2	441	378·0	227·1	501	429·4	258·0	561	480·9	288·9
322	276·0	165·8	382	327·4	196·7	442	378·9	227·6	502	430·3	258·5	562	481·7	289·5
323	276·9	166·4	383	328·3	197·3	443	379·7	228·2	503	431·2	259·1	563	482·6	290·0
324	277·7	166·9	384	329·2	197·8	444	380·6	228·7	504	432·0	259·6	564	483·4	290·5
325	278·6	167·4	385	330·0	198·3	445	381·4	229·2	505	432·9	260·1	565	484·3	291·0
326	279·4	167·9	386	330·9	198·8	446	382·3	229·7	506	433·7	260·6	566	485·2	291·5
327	280·3	168·4	387	331·7	199·3	447	383·2	230·2	507	434·6	261·1	567	486·0	292·0
328	281·2	168·9	388	332·6	199·8	448	384·0	230·7	508	435·4	261·6	568	486·9	292·5
329	282·0	169·4	389	333·4	200·3	449	384·9	231·3	509	436·3	262·2	569	487·7	293·1
330	282·9	170·0	390	334·3	200·9	450	385·7	231·8	510	437·2	262·7	570	488·6	293·6
331	283·7	170·5	391	335·2	201·4	451	386·6	232·3	511	438·0	263·2	571	489·4	294·1
332	284·6	171·0	392	336·0	201·9	452	387·4	232·8	512	438·9	263·7	572	490·3	294·6
333	285·4	171·5	393	336·9	202·4	453	388·3	233·3	513	439·7	264·2	573	491·2	295·1
334	286·3	172·0	394	337·7	202·9	454	389·2	233·8	514	440·6	264·7	574	492·0	295·6
335	287·2	172·5	395	338·6	203·4	455	390·0	234·3	515	441·4	265·2	575	492·9	296·1
336	288·0	173·1	396	339·4	204·0	456	390·9	234·9	516	442·3	265·8	576	493·7	296·7
337	288·9	173·6	397	340·3	204·5	457	391·7	235·4	517	443·2	266·3	577	494·6	297·2
338	289·7	174·1	398	341·2	205·0	458	392·6	235·9	518	444·0	266·8	578	495·4	297·7
339	290·6	174·6	399	342·0	205·5	459	393·4	236·4	519	444·9	267·3	579	496·3	298·2
340	291·4	175·1	400	342·9	206·0	460	394·3	236·9	520	445·7	267·8	580	497·2	298·7
341	292·3	175·6	401	343·7	206·5	461	395·2	237·4	521	446·6	268·3	581	498·0	299·2
342	293·2	176·1	402	344·6	207·0	462	396·0	237·9	522	447·4	268·8	582	498·9	299·8
343	294·0	176·7	403	345·4	207·6	463	396·9	238·5	523	448·3	269·4	583	499·7	300·3
344	294·9	177·2	404	346·3	208·1	464	397·7	239·0	524	449·2	269·9	584	500·6	300·8
345	295·7	177·7	405	347·2	208·6	465	398·6	239·5	525	450·0	270·4	585	501·4	301·3
346	296·6	178·2	406	348·0	209·1	466	399·4	240·0	526	450·9	270·9	586	502·3	301·8
347	297·4	178·7	407	348·9	209·6	467	400·3	240·5	527	451·7	271·4	587	503·2	302·3
348	298·3	179·2	408	349·7	210·1	468	401·2	241·0	528	452·6	271·9	588	504·0	302·8
349	299·2	179·7	409	350·6	210·7	469	402·2	241·6	529	453·4	272·5	589	504·9	303·4
350	300·0	180·3	410	351·4	211·2	470	402·9	242·1	530	454·3	273·0	590	505·7	303·9
351	300·9	180·8	411	352·3	211·7	471	403·7	242·6	531	455·2	273·5	591	506·6	304·4
352	301·7	181·3	412	353·2	212·2	472	404·6	243·1	532	456·0	274·0	592	507·4	304·9
353	302·6	181·8	413	354·0	212·7	473	405·4	243·6	533	456·9	274·5	593	508·3	305·4
354	303·4	182·3	414	354·9	213·2	474	406·3	244·1	534	457·7	275·0	594	509·2	305·9
355	304·3	182·8	415	355·7	213·7	475	407·2	244·6	535	458·6	275·5	595	510·0	306·4
356	305·2	183·4	416	356·6	214·3	476	408·0	245·2	536	459·4	276·1	596	510·9	307·0
357	306·0	183·9	417	357·4	214·8	477	408·9	245·7	537	460·3	276·6	597	511·7	307·5
358	306·9	184·4	418	358·3	215·3	478	409·7	246·2	538	461·2	277·1	598	512·6	308·0
359	307·7	184·9	419	359·2	215·8	479	410·6	246·7	539	462·0	277·6	599	513·4	308·5
360	308·6	185·4	420	360·0	216·3	480	411·4	247·2	540	462·9	278·1	600	514·3	309·0
Dist	Dep.	D.Lat	Dist	Dep.	D.Lat	Dist	Dep.	D.Lat	Dist	Dep.	D.Lat	Dist	Dep.	D.Lat
D Lon		Dep.	D Lon		Dep.	D Lon		Dep.	D Lon		Dep.	D Lon		Dep.

Practice work.

1. D.Lat, D.Long, M.Lat (pages 167, 634, 765)
Find the D.Lat, D.Long and M.Lat of a ship sailing between the following positions:

(a) From 35°17.3′N   22°18.3′W   to   30°15.1′N   19°03.1′W
(b) From   5°17.0′N   1°13.4′E   to   3°14.0′S   1°10.4′W
(c) From 34°14.0′S 179°18.4′W   to   40°03.0′S 176°17.9′E
(d) From 49°35.0′N   17°18.0′E   to   47°30.0′N   13°14.0′E
(e) From   9°12.0′N   17°32.0′W   to   7°13.0′S   24°13.0′W

2. Converting D.Long to Departure (pages 734, 421)
Find the Departure for a D.Long of 250′ at the following Mean Latitudes:
(a) At M.Lat 30°00′
(b) At M.Lat 61°00′
(c) At M.Lat 29°30′
(d) At M.Lat 30°45′
(e) At M.Lat 60°15′

3. Converting Departure to D.Long (pages 734, 421)
Find the D.Long for a Departure of 300 miles at the following Mean Latitudes:
(a) At M.Lat 59°00′
(b) At M.Lat 30°30′
(c) At M.Lat 29°15′
(d) At M.Lat 60°00′
(e) At M.Lat 61°00′

4. Quadrants of the Compass (page 217)
Express the following True Course readings in quadrantal terms:
(a) 015°
(b) 093°
(c) 187°
(d) 269°
(e) 271°

5. Finding True Course and Distance (page 987)
At 0800 hours on June 6th, a ship leaves a position 33°15′N   21°05′W and sails to a position 24°45′N   26°55′W. Its average speed is 7 knots (7 nautical miles per hour). Calculate:
(a) True Course
(b) Distance
(c) Date and time of arrival

6. Finding the new position (page 895)
A ship leaves a position 29°45′N   160°05′E and sails for 30 hours at an average speed of 10 knots along a True Course of 060°. Calculate the new position.

Practice work answers.

1. (a) D.Lat: 302.2′S D.Long: 195.2′E M.Lat: 32°46.2′
   (b) D.Lat: 511.0′S D.Long: 143.8′W M.Lat: 1°01.5′
   (c) D.Lat: 349.0′S D.Long: 263.7′W M.Lat: 37°08.5′
   (d) D.Lat: 125.0′S D.Long: 244.0′W M.Lat: 48°32.5′
   (e) D.Lat: 985.0′S D.Long: 401.0′W M.Lat: 8°12.5′

2. (a) 216.5 miles
   (b) 121.2 miles
   (c) 217.6 miles
   (d) 214.85 miles
   (e) 124.05 miles

3. (a) 582′
   (b) 348.25′
   (c) 343.9′
   (d) 600′
   (e) 619′

4. (a) N15°E
   (b) S87°E
   (c) S7°W
   (d) S89°W
   (e) N89°W

5. (a) 211°
   (b) 595 miles
   (c) 2100 hours, June 9th

6.   Lat: 32°15′N
      Long: 165°08′E

Index